The Goldman Guide to Medical Jurisprudence and Medical Ethics

Written and Prepared by

David Eckstein Goldman, JD, DO, FCLM
Physician/Psychiatrist/Attorney At Law

Board Certified General Psychiatry
Board Certified Forensic Psychiatry
Associate Clinical Professor Southern Illinois University School of Medicine
[Department of Medical Humanities]
Assistant Professor ATSU/Kirksville College of Osteopathic Medicine
[Department of Neurobehavioral Sciences]

Attorney At Law
Member of the Illinois and Missouri Bar
Fellow in the American College of Legal Medicine
Associate Clinical Professor Southern Illinois University School of Medicine
[Department of Medical Humanities]

MP
Miracle Press

The Goldman Guide to Medical Jurisprudence and Medical Ethics

Written by:
David Eckstein Goldman, JD, DO, FCLM
Physician/Psychiatrist/Attorney At Law

© Copyright 2014, David Eckstein Goldman, All Rights Reserved

No part of this publication may be reproduced, distributed or transmitted in any form or by any means, including photocopying, recording, or other electronic or mechanical methods, without the prior written permission of the publisher, except in the case of brief quotations embodied in critical reviews and certain other non-commercial uses permitted by copyright law.

Published by:
Miracle Press
P. O. Box 765
Jacksonville, Illinois 62651
www.thegoldmangroup.org

Cover design and interior layout: www.TheBookProducer.com
Printed in the United States of America

ISBN: 978-0-9774185-2-7

Welcome to Medical Jurisprudence and Medical Ethics. This is a journey into that area where medicine and the law intersect. It is the purpose of this book to familiarize you with the following concepts:

American Legal and Judicial System	Informed Consent
Bioethics	Malingering
Burden of Proof	Malpractice
Competence and Capacity	Malpractice Insurance
Contract Law	Medical Records
Courtroom Testimony	Privacy and Confidentiality
HIPAA	Risk Management

CONTENTS

About the Author 7

Introduction   The American Legal and Judicial System 9

Chapter 1   Bioethics and Medical Jurisprudence 23

Chapter 2   Elements of Malpractice 28

Chapter 3   Informed Consent 44

Chapter 4   Medical Records 61

Chapter 5   The Physician-Patient Relationship 66

Chapter 6   Medical Malpractice Insurance 69

Chapter 7   Issues in Risk Management 73

Chapter 8   HIPAA: To Be or Not to Be (included) 78

Chapter 9   Guidelines for Courtroom Testimony 81

Chapter 10   Malingering 87

Chapter 11   Competence and Capacity 97

Chapter 12   Contract Law 101

Index 111

ABOUT THE AUTHOR

Dr. Goldman graduated from the University of Illinois in Champaign-Urbana, Illinois, in 1973, having received his Bachelor of Arts Degree with a major in History, a focus in Religious Studies, and a double minor in Psychology and Sociology. After completing his undergraduate studies, Dr.Goldman attended Washington University School of Law, receiving his Juris Doctorate Degree in 1976. From 1976 until beginning medical school in 1987, he served as secretary-treasurer and corporate legal counsel for Central Industries, Inc.

In 1987, Dr. Goldman entered medical school at the Kirksville College of Osteopathic Medicine, graduating in 1991 with his Doctor of Osteopathy degree. He completed a traditional transitional rotating internship at the Kirksville Osteopathic Medical Center in Kirksville, Missouri, in 1992, after which time he began his residency training in Psychiatry at Vanderbilt University Medical Center in Nashville, Tennessee. Dr. Goldman completed his residency training in 1996, and completed his Fellowship training in Child and Adolescent Psychiatry in 1997, also at Vanderbilt University Medical Center.

After completing his Residency and Fellowship training, Dr. Goldman returned to Springfield, Illinois, establishing his practice in psychiatry. He is the Medical Director for The Goldman Group, LLC, and serves as a medicolegal consultant, as well as continuing his private psychotherapy and psychopharmacology management practice. He also serves as a professor at both Southern Illinois University Medical School in Springfield, Illinois, and at ATSU/Kirksville College of Osteopathic Medicine in Kirksville, Missouri.

Dr. Goldman was the 2001 recipient of the Max Gutensohn *Professor of the Year Award* at Kirksville College of Osteopathic Medicine, and in 2001 was also awarded the *Order of Merlin Shield* by the International Brotherhood of Magicians. In 2007, he was one of 18 psychiatrists selected from among the nation's physicians to receive the NAMI *Exemplary Psychiatrist Award* presented at the international meeting of the American Psychiatric Association.

INTRODUCTION

The American Legal and Judicial System

The American Legal System was developed to bring order out of chaos and civility to an uncivilized way of settling disputes. The older concept of trial by combat gave way to trial by law, with the new combatants being the attorneys, the new combat arena being the courtroom.

The arbiters of the dispute are the judge, who is the trier of law, and the jury, the trier of fact. Civil trials usually result in the payment of monetary damages, although other remedies may be ordered such as requiring a party to refrain from a certain action (an injunction) or requiring a party to perform a certain action (specific performance). For the legal system to work, there must be a competent authority from whom the law is derived (the Government) and the law must be capable of being enforced. The law is derived from the power that is inherent in the authorized body. The power may be exercised in the form of democracy, republic, monarchy, dictatorship, or totalitarian state. The division of that power may be in the hands of a country, state, county, city, or town.

Where does the power come from that becomes the government? Government is actually the result of the transfer of rights/power. It is the transfer of rights/power from the people, the citizenry, based upon the principle that the benefits derived from safety and stability are commensurate with the rights surrendered to create the body that will provide and guarantee that safety and stability. In the United States, individuals have relinquished certain rights for a government that functions as a dual form: federal and state. These two governments are given their power via enabling documents we call constitutions. These constitutions are legal documents that embody the rights of the citizens as managed by the government and also designate the restraints that limit the power of that government.

CONSTITUTIONS

Just as the United States Constitution was adopted and ratified as a part of the founding of this nation, so too each state has its own Constitution that was adopted at the time of statehood. Each of these Constitutions defines the tripartite being of the Federal and State governments. Just as the human being is mind/body/spirit, id/ego/superego, so too are our governments Executive/Legislative/Judicial. The major dichotomy is that between Federal and State powers. The Federal government has exclusive powers in matters relating to:

- Citizenship
- Immigration
- Interstate commerce
- Maintaining an army and waging war
- National form of money ("to coin money")
- National taxation and spending
- Naturalization
- The postal system

All powers not specifically delegated to the Federal government, are reserved to the States [10th Amendment].

The Constitution of the United States was created so that it could be amended. Article V of the Constitution so states. The process

Introduction: The American Legal and Judicial System

was made intentionally cumbersome so as not to be abused. The process requires:

- Two-thirds vote of both houses of Congress; or
- National convention called by Congress on application of two thirds of the state legislatures.

The Amendment then becomes effective on the date that three fourths of the states have ratified the Amendment.

As of 2014, the Constitution has been amended 26 times. With the exception of the 18th Amendment (*Prohibition*) which was repealed by the 21st Amendment, all of the Amendments are still operative.

The U.S. Constitution is the Supreme Law of the Land. This is carefully stated in Article VI, Section 2:

This Constitution, and the laws of the United States which shall be made in pursuance thereof; and all treaties made, or which shall be made, under the authority of the United States, shall be the supreme law of the land; and the judges in every state shall be bound thereby, anything in the Constitution or laws of any State to the contrary notwithstanding.

This is important because when combined with both of the concepts of *precedent* and *stare decisis* we understand that decisions made at the Federal Level, both by Federal District Courts and by the United States Supreme Court are binding upon the states, meaning, binding upon us in whatever jurisdiction we happen to be practicing medicine or law at the moment.

Please keep in mind that constitutions, statutes, administrative law, legislatures and court systems come in two flavors: State and Federal. Remember that both state and federal systems are tripartite:

Executive, Legislative, and Judicial. Remember that legislatures, both state and federal, are bipartite or bicameral: a house of representatives and a senate.

What are Constitutional Rights? These are individual liberties granted by the state or federal constitution to the citizens of each state or of the United States and are protected from governmental interference or denial.

What are Statutes? Statutes are acts of a state or federal legislature (the House and the Senate), adopted under the authority granted by the relevant constitution, according to the means and format elaborated by that relevant Constitution so that the act becomes the law that governs conduct within its scope. Statutes define required civil conduct, define criminal behavior, set punishment(s) for criminal acts, create inferior governmental bodies, effect taxation and allot spending of public funds, and are the extensions of the relevant legislature to promote the general welfare of the constituents. In plain English: statutes are the laws passed by state and federal government that regulate the lives of citizens and businesses.

What is Administrative Law? In order to actually function, the government is divided into many agencies created by statutes written and passed by our legislatures (state and federal), signed into law by the requisite executive (governor or US President) and these created agencies are given authority to regulate the activities for which they were created. For example, in order to protect our land, water and air, the government has created the Environmental Protection Agency (remember, there are a Federal EPA and individual State EPA's). In order to perform its function, the EPA has been granted a limited police power: it may create rules and regulations and may enforce these with threat of fines and restraining orders. Some agencies are given limited jurisdiction (control) to hear cases in a more relaxed judicial-like setting with a hearing commissioner (an administrative judge) who makes decisions that are enforceable as administrative laws. In concise terms: legislatures pass enabling statutes that create an agency and enable it to promulgate rules and regulations that govern the subject matter within the agency's authority. When the agency promulgates its rules and regulations in conformity with the enabling statutes, its rules and regulations have the same force of law as if enacted by the legislature itself. Challenges to the regulations may be made in Court. However, if it is established that the agency has acted within the lawful scope of its powers and has not acted arbitrarily with regard to any individual, Courts are generally foreclosed from reviewing the merits of the agency's decision. The decision is thus binding.

What is Common Law? The concept of Common Law is found in the words themselves. Common law developed in England prior to legislative law. Common law refers to judge-made rules prior to statutes being made to regulate specific human experiences. It wasn't until the year 1195, during the reign of Henry II, that English Court decisions were formalized into permanent written records. These written decisions accumulated over the centuries. In this evolutionary process decisions rendered based on a given set of facts came to be applied to newer cases when they presented similar facts and situations. Thus the decision in a case set the precedent for future cases with the same fact scenario. This established the cornerstone of the common law: *stare decisis* – "let the decision stand." This concept is the foundation of the stability of the law: citizens could (can and should) expect similar treatment in similar circumstances. Historically, as the newly formed American nation evolved after the Revolution, the states feared that the National/Central government would establish a central common law that would abuse the rights of the states and thus limitations on the jurisdiction and powers of the newly established Federal Courts were put in place:

- Federal judges were not allowed to make law (English judges actually made law – in America that power was given to the Legislature); Federal judges were instead empowered only to interpret and apply the existing law.
- If Federal law were not at issue, the case was/is to be heard in a state court with one main exception: diversity of citizenship/conflict of law. What does that mean? That means that if the issue at hand is between citizens of two separate states, the case may be brought into Federal Court. However, the Federal judge must render a decision that conforms to both state common law and state statutory law.

What is Full Faith and Credit? Recognizing that different states may deal with issues in different ways, our Founding Fathers wanted to provide that a judgment duly rendered in one state would be honored in another. Hence the US Constitution contains Article IV, Section I. In order for a judgment in one state to be enforceable in another, the following criteria must be met:

- The state court rendering the judgment must have jurisdiction to hear the case.
- The judgment must be final.
- The judgment must have been based on the merits of the case (meaning, the decision must have been rendered based on the issue in controversy).

THE JUDICIAL SYSTEM

Our judicial or court system is based in the common law and is noted for two distinct characteristics.

1) Our judicial system is an adversarial system that is considered *friendly*. What makes the American jurisprudential system friendly? It is the friendly concept of discovery. Discovery is the

Introduction: The American Legal and Judicial System

modern pretrial procedure whereby the parties to the action are able to gain information held by the adverse party. Common types of discovery are:

- Depositions
- Interrogatories [written questions]
- Production of documents
- Requests for admissions

> Eg: John buys a new motorcycle manufactured by Heapojunk Corporation. On his first day of riding, the front brake does not engage resulting in John hitting a vehicle in front of him. Via discovery John is able to access documents, memos, and test run results from the manufacturer with regard to the motorcycle's design and performance that are essential to his product liability law suit against the manufacturer.

2) Our judicial system is consistent, stable, and dependable via continuity from appellate decisions due to the concepts of precedent and stare decisis:

> Precedent: a previously decided case is recognized as the standard for the resolution of future cases.

> Stare Decisis: [Latin – *to stand by that which was decided*] Rule by which courts stand on principles announced in a previous decision and rely upon the judicial precedent as the guide to deciding new cases raising issues similar to the prior case(s).

Our legal system is based on the following premise: for every wrong there should be a remedy. Hence we have created a forum for our legal disputes to be heard and decisions rendered: our courts. The court system is divided into State and Federal. Both systems are divided into:

- Trial courts
- Courts of appeal
- Supreme Court(s)

The trial court is typically the entry level to the judicial system. It is here that testimony is heard and evidence presented. The material of the case is heard either by a judge or a jury – the trier of fact. If there is a jury, the judge then focuses on the role of trier of law: he/she interprets the applicable law in the case and explains it to the jury for them to apply that law to the facts. The judge presents to the jury instructions informing them of the law applicable to the case, to guide them in reaching a verdict according to law and the evidence. An instruction to the jury is a charge to the jury, more a command than a request.

The appellate court (court of appeals) is different from the trial court in that it does NOT hear facts and witnesses as the trial court does. The appellate court hears legal arguments. These legal arguments relate to the validity of the decision of the trial court. No new evidence is introduced. The higher court, the appeals court, is limited to considering whether the lower court erred on a question of law or rendered a decision contrary to the evidence presented during the trial.

In the trial court, there is only one judge. In the appeals court, there will be from 3 to 9 judges, and the ruling of the appellate court is based on a majority vote. If a tie vote occurs, the trial court's ruling is upheld. The decisions made by appellate courts are written as opinions and published in books called reporters. These published decisions comprise the body of law and legal principles of the American Common Law. These reported decisions are a matter of public record and are available in public libraries.

In most jurisdictions, the highest appellate court is the State Supreme Court. It is usually the appellate state court of last resort, and,

Introduction: The American Legal and Judicial System

in the absence of a federal question, the decision handed down in the state supreme court is final. In some states the final court of appeal is not called the supreme court. For the Federal Court system, the United States Supreme Court is the final arbiter. It is provided for in the US Constitution and consists of one Chief Justice and eight Associate Justices, all appointed by the US President upon approval by the US Senate. While the Supreme Court is the ultimate appellate court, it is granted original jurisdiction in certain specified areas: cases involving ambassadors, other public ministers and consuls, and in cases where a state is a party to the dispute.

Let's look again at the courts. Remember there are two systems – state and federal. Both are created by Constitution: the state courts by each of the states' respective constitutions and the federal courts by the US Constitution.

Federal Courts

The Federal Court System. The federal courts are courts of limited jurisdiction: they may make decisions only in those cases dealing with specific subject matter. Federal courts are limited by the jurisdiction specified in the US Constitution and as legislated by the US Congress. Article III of the US Constitution focuses specifically on the issue of federal judicial power. Section 2 of Article III details the specified areas of jurisdiction of the federal courts:

- Admiralty and maritime cases
- Cases affecting ambassadors, public ministers, consuls
- Cases arising under the US Constitution, US Laws, US Treaties
- Controversies to which the United States is a party
- Controversies between two or more states
- Controversies between a state and a citizen of a different state
- Controversies between citizens of different states

- Controversies between citizens of the same state claiming lands under grants of different states
- Controversies between a state or its citizen(s) and a foreign state or its citizen(s)

Federal District Courts. The US is divided into 91 federal judicial districts. Each federal district has its own district court. Other than the District Court for Wyoming, which includes Wyoming plus those parts of Yellowstone national Park that extend into Montana and Idaho, federal judicial districts do NOT extend across state lines. Because some states are geographically large and populous, they may have more than one judicial district and thus more than one district court: e.g. California, New York, Texas. Remember, the federal district courts are the federal trial courts. Unless designated otherwise by the US Constitution or Congressional law, these courts are courts of original jurisdiction for federal cases, and no controversy or appeal may be heard in a federal appeals court unless it has been first adjudicated in a district court.

Federal Appeals Courts. The federal appeals court system consists of 11 courts: one for the District of Columbia and 10 others. Each federal appeals court has jurisdiction over between 3 and 10 state judicial districts. While these federal courts of appeal serve primarily as forums of appeal for cases tried in lower courts (federal district courts), they do retain some areas of original jurisdiction, the most notable being review of decisions made by the many federal administrative agencies (remember earlier when we talked about administrative law).

The Supreme Court. The United States Supreme Court is provided for in Article III, Section 1 of the US Constitution. While its size has varied from 6 to 10 members throughout history, in 1869 its current number of 9 justices was established. As mentioned earlier, other than a specified set of exceptions, the Supreme Court serves an appellate function. There is no appeal from a decision rendered

Introduction: The American Legal and Judicial System

by this Court (although this Court may agree to rehear a case – e.g.: the Tarasoff case). If this Court interprets a statute or law that proves to be at odds with Congress' plans, Congress' only right of redress is to rewrite the statute.

Other Federal Courts. There are several other federal courts just to be aware of –
Court of Claims: hears claims against the United States (1855)
Court of Customs and Patent Appeals (1909)
Tax Court (1969)

State Courts

These courts are established by state constitution and by state law (legislation). These courts have general jurisdiction to hear cases arising under state law and to hear the complaints of the citizens of that state. All states provide for a multilevel system of courts. While it may vary from state to state, the Michigan model is fairly representative:

Supreme Court (top of the pyramid)
Court of Appeals

- Circuit Courts: general trial courts empowered to hear all matters of law, equity and appeals concerning state administrative agency actions.
- District Courts: general jurisdiction courts that hear controversies of amounts less than $10,000. (These courts were established in Michigan by legislative action to help relieve the burden on the Circuit Courts.)
- Small Claims Court: a division of the District Courts that hears claims for less than $6000; less formal setting.
- Probate Court: specialized court to probate wills, deal with juvenile problems, adoption proceedings and other areas of family law.
- Court of Claims: claims against the state and its agents.

Tenure. The literal meaning is *right to hold* and it refers to an official's term in office. For *federal judges*, unless they have engaged in malfeasance (wrongful acts), they are tenured for life. *State judges* tend to be elected officials for a fixed term.

The concept of the Burden of Proof. In our legal system, once an action is brought, the question of the facts, the evidence, and will the jury or judge find for the person claiming injury, or the state who is bringing an action against an individual for criminal acts, is determined by the burden of proof: the amount of evidence necessary to prove or disprove the case. There are three levels of proof:

- Preponderance of the evidence: this is the level of evidentiary burden and degree of proof that will lead the trier of fact to find that the existence of the fact in issue is more probable than not. It refers to a finding of >51% for the party going forward.
- Clear and convincing evidence: this is the level of evidentiary burden and degree of proof that will lead the trier of fact to find that the fact in issue is greater than a mere preponderance of the evidence yet less than beyond a reasonable doubt or between 70% and 80% most likely to have occurred.
- Beyond a reasonable doubt: this is the degree of certainty and burden of proof required for a juror to make a legally valid determination of the guilt of a criminal defendant. These words are used in instructions to the jury in a criminal trial to indicate that innocence is to be presumed unless the jury can see no reasonable doubt of the guilt of the person charged. The term does not require that proof be so clear that no possibility of error exists; it means that the evidence must be so conclusive that all reasonable doubts are removed from the mind of the ordinary person: evidentiary finding >90%.

Introduction: The American Legal and Judicial System

Subpoena. Information is the key to any courtroom proceeding, to any legal action. In the course of preparing and litigating a legal case, it becomes necessary to access witnesses and to access documents in the possession of witnesses or other involved individuals. To bring someone to court to testify, or to bring documents to court, a subpoena may be served upon an individual.

Subpoena is Latin for *under penalty*. A subpoena is a legal order issued by judicial authority to compel a person to do something. It is issued by a court or other competent officer or body having authority to adjudicate or render judgment in a controversy. A subpoena is *served* by the sheriff or other officer authorized to execute it. A subpoena may be issued under authority of a court to compel the appearance of a witness at a judicial proceeding.

Subpoena Ad Testificandum is a subpoena to testify. This is the technical name for the ordinary subpoena.

Subpoena Duces Tecum translates into under *penalty you shall bring it with you*. This type of subpoena is issued by a court at the request of one of the parties to a legal suit. A witness having under his/her control documents relevant to the controversy is commanded or instructed to bring such items to court during the trial or to a deposition. A deposition is a method of pretrial discovery that consists of a stenographically transcribed statement of a witness under oath, in response to an attorney's questions, with opportunity for the opposing party or his/her attorney to be present and to cross-examine. Such a statement is the most common form of discovery and may be taken of any witness (whether or not a party to the action). When taken in the form described, it is called an oral deposition.

Contempt. Contempt is an act or failure to act that is perceived by the Court as impeding the process of justice. Failure to comply with a subpoena may be punishable as contempt of court. *Direct Contempt* takes place openly and in the presence of the court. *Constructive Contempt* occurs outside the court, an example is failure to comply with court orders. *Civil Contempt* consists of failure to do something ordered by the court for the benefit of another party to the proceedings; *Criminal Contempt* includes acts disrespectful of the court or its processes that obstruct administration of justice. As a general rule: An order of a court must be obeyed or appealed. It may NOT be disregarded.

Discovery. Discovery is a modern pretrial procedure by which one party gains information held by the adverse party, concerning the case; the disclosure by the adverse party of facts, deeds, and documents that are exclusively within his/her possession or knowledge and that are necessary to support the other party's position. Common types of discovery are depositions, interrogatories, production of documents and requests for admissions.

Interrogatories are used in civil actions. Interrogatories are a pretrial discovery tool in which one party's written questions are served on the adversary, who must provide written replies under oath. Interrogatories can only be served on parties to the action, and while not as flexible as depositions, which include opportunity of cross-examination, they are regarded as a good and inexpensive means of establishing important facts held by the adversary.

CHAPTER 1

Bioethics and Medical Jurisprudence

The concept of bioethics was initiated in mid-1980 by Tom L. Beauchamp and James Childress, who developed the four basic principles that guide in the resolution of bioethical dilemmas [*Principles of Biomedical Ethics* (1985)]:

- Autonomy
- Beneficence
- Nonmaleficence
- Justice

AUTONOMY

The word autonomy is derived from the Greek *auto nomos* meaning self-rule. It is the essence of the concept of freedom of choice, or what in the Western World is considered *liberty*. Applied to medicine, the concept of auto nomos [autonomy] relates to the physician's duty to respect the free choice exercised by the patient. Hence, the patient, is the true captain of his/her ship, and the master of his/her soul. Justice Benjamin Cardozo summed this up best in 1914, in the decision in the case of Schloendorf v Society of New York Hospital (1914 105N.E.92 [NYCA]) when he wrote:

> *Every human being of adult years and sound mind has a right to determine what shall be done with his own body.*

In practical terms, for one to exercise decisions with true self-rule, it is critical that patients receive the requisite information upon which to base a rational, well thought out choice. Thus, the legal concept of informed consent and the correlate of informed refusal (note *Truman v Thomas* California Supreme Court, 1980) both derive from the concept of autonomy. It is important to keep in mind that medicine is based upon the precept of allowing autonomy, the freedom to make decisions about one's own body, whereas law is about limiting autonomy: there must be limits on purely autonomous decision making when the rights of others are affected. Hence the legal aphorism:

Your rights end where my nose begins.

Also keep in mind the legal aphorism:

One must take one's plaintiff as one finds him.

Thus the law intervenes to limit autonomy to the extent that we must protect the rights of each individual as he or she is situated. Essentially: *to each according to his needs, from each according to his abilities* [Karl Marx, 1875]. What does all of this verbiage mean? We must allow patients the autonomy to make decisions about their own bodies for so long as they are mentally competent to make such decisions once they have received the information necessary to make an informed decision; this thus requires health care providers to explain the information in details that the patient is able to understand. In the words of Justice Cardozo the patient should meet two important criteria:

- Be of adult years
- Be of sound mind

Some patients will have advocates/guardians and some will have those who have been given power of attorney to represent the patient's best interests. It is important for health care providers to have such documents in hand evidencing the authority of another person to stand in as the patient's surrogate decision-maker when allowing *substituted judgment* to be exercised. It is important to keep in mind that the individual should express his/her health wishes while cogent, coherent, and competent so that these desires will be followed when he/she is not conscious, coherent, or no longer competent – hence the concept of the advance directive, living will, and power of attorney (see p. 27).

Also arising out of this concept of autonomy is the concept of *privacy/confidentiality*. Remember that the patient is the one owning the privilege of privacy/confidentiality with regard to his/her diagnosis/treatment. The patient may waive his/her right to confidentiality. We as health care providers may NOT waive/surrender the patient's right without his/her written consent (see p. 32).

BENEFICENCE/NONMALEFICENCE

In the Hippocratic Oath, the physician swears:

> *I will follow that system or regimen which according to my ability and judgment I consider for the benefit of my patients and abstain from whatever is deleterious and mischievous.*

As a corollary, all medical students are taught the first principle of medicine:

> Primum Non Nocere (*Above all else, do no harm*)

It is the purpose of medicine and the goal of the physician to alleviate pain and suffering, to provide comfort and to bring about healing. Hence, the role of the physician is to behave with beneficence (the act of being kind or doing good) and to avoid maleficence (wrongdoing or misconduct).

In reviewing the concepts of beneficence and maleficence, the physician must be aware of when interventions may be futile and defer to patient autonomy to discern when an intervention may actually become an act of maleficence if instead of relieving suffering, alleviating pain and providing a cure, the treatment is merely for the educational purpose of the physician, or to assuage the physician's feelings of hopelessness and helplessness.

JUSTICE

The issue of justice is that of fair play. It is the concept of justice that focuses on the equitable distribution of health care services. The AMA Council on Ethical and Judicial Affairs, Ethical Considerations in the Allocation of Organs and Other Scarce Medical Resources Among Patients [155 Archives of Internal Medicine 401 (1995)] addresses this issue as follows:

Acceptable Criteria for Resource Allocation Among Patients

Acceptable criteria used to determine the appropriate allocation of resources include the following:

- Likelihood of benefit to the patient
- Improvement in the patient's quality of life
- Duration of benefit
- Urgency of the patient's condition
- Amount of resources needed for successful treatment

ADVANCE DIRECTIVES. An advance directive is a document in which you give instructions about your health care, what you want done or not done, if you can't speak for yourself.

Advance directives are not complicated. They can be short, simple statements expressing your values and choices.

A *health care directive* is a type of advance directive that tells your doctor and your family members what kind of care you would like to have if you become unable to make medical decisions. It is called an *advance directive* because you choose your medical care before you become seriously ill. A health care directive is not limited to cases of "terminal illness." If you cannot make or communicate decisions because of a temporary or permanent illness or injury, a health care directive helps you keep control over health care decisions that are important to you. In your health care directive, you state your wishes about any aspect of your health care, including decisions about life-sustaining treatment.

A *living will* (also known as a *healthcare directive* or *directive to physicians*) is a document that expresses a person's desires and preferences about medical treatment in case he or she becomes unable to communicate these instructions during *terminal illness or permanent unconsciousness (vegetative state)*.

A *durable power of attorney* is the selection of an individual to serve as the patient's advocate when the patient is no longer able to make health care decisions for him or herself. The durable power of attorney can perform some of the functions of a living will. A durable power of attorney differs from a living will in that it may direct the attorney-in-fact to carry out the living will's instructions or it may allow the attorney-in-fact to use his or her own judgment. A durable power of attorney may be used whenever the individual granting the power cannot make his or her own health care decisions; it does not depend on terminal illness or permanent unconsciousness to become effective.

CHAPTER 2

Elements of Malpractice

It is important to keep in mind, as physicians, that we live in a very litigious society. What does this mean to us? It means that in today's changing environment, patients have become *consumers*, physicians have become *providers*, and when a consumer is dissatisfied with the result of his/her received services, he/she might consult a plaintiff's attorney to receive the analogue to a refund for the services received: a malpractice suit. As frightening as this all seems, it is important to remember that only one in twenty injured patients brings an action in malpractice.

When talking about litigation, remember, ANYBODY CAN SUE ANYBODY ELSE. The key question is CAN THEY PREVAIL? and if so, then comes the all important question, CAN THEY COLLECT? Let us look at the concept of malpractice.

Medical Malpractice lawsuits can be based upon many theories. The most common action for malpractice is based upon the concept of negligence.

Malpractice is essentially based upon the 4 D's:

- Duty
- Dereliction (of that duty: breach)
- Direct Causation (of the injury due to dereliction of duty: proximate cause)
- Damages

Elements of Malpractice

DUTY

The first issue is one of duty. Does some one owe a duty? Who owes a duty to whom? In this instance, we are talking about the legal issues surrounding the provision of professional medical care provided by the physician to the patient. Thus, YOU owe a duty to the patient. What is the duty you owe? Well, you owe the duty of due care. What does that mean? That means essentially that you are to perform your responsibility as a physician with the diligence of due care: you are expected to exercise the degree of skill ordinarily used under similar circumstances by a similar professional.

DERELICTION OF DUTY: BREACH

The second issue is have you breached that duty? Have you been derelict in your performance of that duty? And was that dereliction a negligent failure to act (omission) or a negligent act (commission)? In breaching that duty, the question asked is "What error was committed, if any?" Essentially there are two types of errors:

> *Error in Fact*: the physician fails to inquire about important facts from the patient with regard to his/her current condition; the physician fails to obtain appropriate lab tests, scans, perform a physical exam; the physician fails to order prior records for review. Note: these errors are very hard to justify in defending against a malpractice lawsuit.

> *Error in Judgment*: this occurs if the physician has gathered the appropriate data and in good faith has come to a medical conclusion, however an untoward result ensues. Note: an error in judgment is acceptable if others would have made the same judgment.

DIRECT CAUSATION (proximate cause)

The third issue that must be addressed is whether or not the negligent commission/omission was the direct cause (proximate cause) of the alleged injury. If the complainant, known as the plaintiff, is able to show that a duty was owed to him/her, and that there was a negligent performance or failure to perform that duty, and that the negligent performance of the duty was the direct cause of the alleged injury, the plaintiff must still show (the fourth issue:) damages. As we know today, juries are very eager to find damages that perhaps in the past were not as easily identifiable or acceptable.

How is the duty owed by a physician to a patient initially defined by the Illinois Courts? The Illinois Courts have adopted §323 of the Restatement 2nd of Torts and applied it to actions involving medical negligence:

> *One who undertakes, gratuitously or for consideration, to render services to another which he should recognize as necessary for the protection of the other's person or things, is subject to liability to the other for physical harm resulting from his failure to exercise reasonable care to perform his undertaking, if:*
>
> *his failure to exercise such care increases the risk of such harm, or the harm is suffered because of the other's reliance upon the undertaking*

DAMAGES

Let us look for a moment at the component of damages. What is the purpose of awarding damages? Damages are awarded in a tort action for the purpose of making the injured person "whole" again or returning the person to the position or condition that existed before the tort. A tort is a wrongful act whether intentional or accidental that results in the injury of another person. As it is generally not possible to reverse the effects from a malpractice injury, public policy provides redress through the awarding of monetary compensation. Thus the legal fiction exists that money will make the injured party whole again. Damages may be awarded to compensate for a myriad of injuries. Damages are awarded to compensate for financial, physical, emotional loss. While categories of damages may vary from jurisdiction to jurisdiction, there are essentially two general areas of damages:

- Compensatory
  - general
  - special
- Punitive

Compensatory Damages

General damages are awarded for non-economic losses, including pain and suffering, mental anguish, grief, and other related emotional complaints without any reference to the specific physical injuries of the particular patient.

Special damages are those that are the actual damages, however not necessarily the inevitable result of the injury caused by the defendant and that follow the injury as foreseeable and natural consequences. Typical types of special damages that are compensated by a monetary judgment include:

- Past and future medical, surgical, hospital, related costs
- Past and future loss of income
- Funeral expenses (in the case of death)

Punitive Damages (exemplary damages)

This type of damage award may be granted in addition to the injured patient's actual losses where a wrong performed was aggravated by special circumstances. Such damages are usually awarded when the defendant's conduct has been intentional, grossly negligent, malicious, violent, fraudulent, or with reckless disregard for the consequences of his or her conduct.

Malpractice versus Ethical Breach

Another issue is: was the action one constituting malpractice or was it an unethical action? There is a big difference between the two. If one is embroiled in a legal suit for malpractice one may still practice one's professional art. If one is embroiled in an issue of unethical behavior, one's license may be suspended or terminated.

What might be an ethical question with regard to medication? What if someone is given samples by the pharmaceutical rep and the practitioner, instead of providing the samples to the patient charges the patient for the samples: actually sells the samples? That would be unethical. Malpractice would be mis-prescribing: a) giving the patient a medication to which the patient is allergic and the prescriber should have known by reviewing previous records or by inquiring of the patient, or b) prescribing too high a dose when other professionals in the same field as a group do not prescribe at that dosing level.

Confidentiality and Malpractice

What about confidentiality? Remember that confidentiality is the mandate that you not discuss the patient with anyone else or release any information without the express permission of the patient. Note that the privilege for confidentiality resides with the patient and he/she may waive that privilege. The right to waive the privilege does NOT belong to the physician or therapist, it belongs only to the patient. When we release information, perhaps about the patient's medication, we are doing so only at the direction of the patient. We are not waiving the privilege, the patient is.

The Learned Intermediary Doctrine

There is another doctrine to keep in mind as a prescribing physician: the learned intermediary doctrine. As a physician, you are the intermediary between the pharmaceutical/manufacturing company and the patient. As such, the manufacturers of prescription medications have a duty to warn YOU, the physician, of dangerous side effects of the medication, and YOU, the physician have the duty to convey the necessary warnings to your patients to whom You prescribe the medication. Thus, since YOU prescribe the medication, You, and not the hospital or pharmacist, have the duty to warn. NOTE: should a pharmacist voluntarily choose to warn a patient of possible dangers of a medication, then he/she voluntarily assumes a duty to do so and must use reasonable care in so doing.

Res Ipsa Loquitur

This is a type of malpractice action that has several different components from the traditional malpractice action:

- No expert is needed to establish the standard of care/duty
- No need to prove dereliction of duty/proximate cause
- The burden of proof shifts from the plaintiff to the defendant

In a case wherein something has happened that ordinarily is not supposed to happen, such as a sponge or instrument being left in the patient's body after surgery, the court looks to the concept of res ipsa loquitur: *the thing speaks for itself.* There are four components of this cause of action that must be present for this type of action to prevail:

- The harm complained of rarely occurs in the absence of negligence
- The situation is under the complete control of the defendant physician (such as the surgical suite)
- The plaintiff (aggrieved patient) did not contribute to the untoward result (no contributory negligence)
- Only the defendant(s) have access to the information as to what happened

In this type of case, the burden of proof shifts to the defendant physician to prove he/she was not negligent (a case of guilty until proven innocent).

Reviewing Malpractice Issues

With regard to medical practice we must be keenly attuned to the following issues:

- Did we make the correct diagnosis?
- Did we explain the possible options for treatment?
- Did the treatment have a successful result?
- Did we prescribe the correct medication or engage in the correct procedure?
- Did the medication/procedure lead to an untoward result/side-effect?
- Did we give the patient the appropriate information to make an informed decision?
- Did we explain clearly the potential for the aggrieved side-effect; did we explain it at all?
- Was our action/inaction negligent?
- Was the complainant actually harmed or was there merely not a satisfactory outcome?

Malpractice Lawsuits Based on Theories Other Than Negligence

As a physician, you may be subjected to a malpractice suit based on theories other than negligence. You may be party to litigation for:

- Abandonment of your patient
- Battery
- Breach of confidentiality
- Breach of contract (or warranty to cure)
- Defamation
- Failure to obtain informed consent
- Failure to report

Elements of Malpractice

- Failure to warn and control
- False imprisonment
- Negligent referrals
- Strict liability for drugs and medical devices
- Vicarious liability

Abandonment

Generally you as an outpatient physician are under no duty to accept a patient into your practice. However, once you have accepted a patient into your practice, once you have created a physician-patient relationship, you have accepted the duty of continuity of care. This means that you must either provide patient access to you in the case of medical need or emergency via pager or a backup physician, or by providing your patients with the understanding and direction that should an emergency ensue he/she is to go to the nearest emergency room and have you notified. Failure to be available to your patient in time of need may result in a lawsuit for abandonment or negligent care. If you should choose to leave the practice you are in or if you disengage from a managed care panel, of if you choose to change your practice or practice style, or if you feel that a patient would be better served by seeing another physician, it is suggested to follow these steps in disengaging from a patient so as to avoid litigation for abandonment:

- Notify the patient that effective within 30 days you will no longer be able to provide the patient with his/her care.
- Inform the patient that during that thirty day period you will provide the necessary medication needs of the patient.
- Inform the patient that should the patient experience an emergency during those thirty days that he/she should go to the nearest ER and have you paged for continuity of care.
- Inform the patient that during that thirty day period he/she should be making arrangements for new care with another physician.

- Inform the patient that any records the patient desires to have transferred to his/her new physician will be so sent provided the patient provides the appropriate signed consent/release of information form.
- While not imperative, you may want to send the above notification to the patient via certified mail with a return receipt requested card.

Battery

Keep in mind that the theory behind this action is NOT one of negligence. This cause of action is based upon the theory of an intentional tort. The law recognizes that individuals are to be free from unwarranted and unwanted intrusion. In legal terms, the touching of an individual without his/her express or implied consent is a battery. The attempt to touch another without consent is an assault. In this instance, the law relies heavily upon the concept of the patient's autonomy or right to have control over his/her own person, thus any medical treatment that the patient claims was not performed with consent, may be claimed as a battery. In a case of battery, there is no need to prove actual harm, only that the intervention was not approved by the patient. The amount of damages of course will relate directly to the amount of harm in most cases. Examples of an action for battery:

- The sexual therapy cases in which therapists have engaged in sexual activity with a patient under the pretext of treatment
- The unauthorized extension of a surgery to" nonconsented" bodily organs unjustified by the original procedure
- The treatment of an individual contrary to his/her religious convictions that limit certain medical procedures

Most jurisdictions at this time have by statute removed the battery theory litigations because of the need for informed consent by patients, and have replaced the old battery theory law suits with law suits for failure to obtain informed consent.

Breach of Confidentiality

Remember that confidentiality is the mandate that you not discuss the patient with anyone else or release any information without the express permission of the patient. Note that the privilege for confidentiality resides with the patient and he/she may waive that privilege. The right to waive the privilege does NOT belong to the physician, it belongs only to the patient. When we release information, perhaps about the patient's medication, we are doing so only at the direction of the patient. We are not waiving the privilege, the patient is. The rules on confidentiality vary from state to state and even with regard to different medical specialties: note that confidentiality with regard to mental health and substance abuse issues is established by statute in the states separately from other medical issues. It is important to be aware of these statutes in the state(s) in which you practice.

Breach of Contract or Warranty to Cure

As a physician, if you make any promises or give any warranties that you will achieve a particular result for a patient or effect a specific cure and the patient submits to the treatment you have recommended, if the result proves to be less than what the patient deems was promised, you may be subject to a lawsuit in contract rather than in tort. The major advantage to a plaintiff in suing for breach of contract instead of medical malpractice is that a medical standard of care need not be shown. The plaintiff need prove only that a promise was made and relied upon and that the promise was not kept and damages resulted from the unkept promise. The plaintiff must prove that he/she was damaged by the physician's breach of promise. While a physician may give a guess as to the possible result of a procedure/surgery/medicational intervention, breach of contract or warranty actions usually arise when the physician sells the patient on a particular surgery or treatment approach. The best approach for the physician is to make clear to the patient that he/she cannot guarantee any specific outcome.

Defamation

A statement is defamatory if it impugns a person's integrity, virtue, and lowers that person in the eyes of the community or causes others in the community to cease from engaging in dealings with the person. A defamatory statement that is a verbal communication is *slander*; when a defamatory statement is made in writing it is *libel*. In the law, truth is an absolute defense to an action for defamation.

If the statement made is true, no action will lie for defamation.

Failure to Obtain Informed Consent

If an untoward result occurs due to a procedure or medication, it is not unlikely that the patient will initiate a lawsuit based on the theory that he/she was not aware of the possible result. As a physician it is imperative that you inform the patient prior to the procedure or initiation of medication or any treatment of the potential risks and side effects in clear understandable terms. It is important that you explain to your patient other alternatives that are available. Failure to do so may result in a law suit for failure to obtain INFORMED consent.

Failure to Report

Every jurisdiction requires the reporting of child abuse: physical, sexual, mental (as it is defined by statute in each state). Each state has reporting requirements as well for sexually transmitted diseases. The physician's failure to comply with the statutory requirements may make him/her liable for criminal penalties. Failure to report has also been held to be negligence per se (not requiring proof of negligence) in civil actions brought by injured third parties. The statutes exempt physicians from liability for breach of confidentiality in the specific areas of reporting.

Elements of Malpractice

Failure to Warn and Control

The failure of a physician to warn the patient or third parties of a foreseeable risk is held to be a negligent act. If the physician is aware of a physical debility in the patient that may put others at risk, he/she is negligent for failure to either warn the patient of this possibility or to make appropriate report (e.g. seizures; see reporting below). If the physician is aware of a danger from a specific medication that puts the patient at risk for falling or being sedated (and making the use of motorized vehicles dangerous to the patient and/or others) the physician is at risk for liability to the patient as well as to potential third party victims. There may also be a duty to warn if the physician is aware of the patient's desire to harm a third party and the physician does not warn the third party or take all action within his/her power to keep the third party safe (*Tarasoff*).

False Imprisonment

False imprisonment is a tort that protects an individual from restraint of movement. This action occurs if an individual is restrained against his/her will in any confined space or area. The plaintiff (aggrieved party) is entitled to be compensated for loss of time, for any inconvenience suffered, for emotional distress, for physical harm, and for any related expenses. This issue arises most commonly in cases of involuntary commitment of patients with mental illness. If a patient is held involuntarily, it is important that as the physician you comply with all pertinent state laws.

Negligent Referrals

Physicians today frequently request consultations from other physicians, especially regarding hospitalized patients. A referring physician usually is not liable for the negligence of the specialist. However, the referring physician may be liable for the referred-to physician's misdeeds if each physician assumes the other will provide certain care that is omitted by both or if they neglect a common duty (e.g.: postoperative care).

Strict Liability for Drugs and Medical Devices

Strict liability is the concept of liability without the need for showing or proving fault. This liability, which is not negligence based, is imposed on manufacturers, sellers, and distributors of unreasonably dangerous and defective products for injuries resulting from their use. Such liability is independent of negligence law, and a defendant's degree of care is irrelevant in lawsuits based on the concept of strict liability. Since every medical device and drug has its potential hazards, manufacturers, sellers and distributors of such products are not held liable for damages if they give adequate warnings about how to avoid the risks and make their products as safe as possible. These warnings must be given clearly, prominently, and in a timely manner, as well as to the proper person. Over-promotion of a product might negate the effect of otherwise adequate warnings. Physicians may be held liable in a medical malpractice suit for his/her failure to inform and adequately warn the patient of a dangerous or defective product in his/her role as a *learned intermediary*.

Vicarious Liability

Vicarious liability is the principle wherein one person is held liable for the wrongful act of another person. This is applicable to physicians when they employ or supervise other health team members that may be less qualified than the physician. Thus physicians are held to owe a duty to their patients to supervise nurses, technicians, and other subordinates within their practice. That duty creates vicarious liability (also know as imputed liability) for the omissions or commissions of another. There are three main doctrines that have been relied upon for the imputing of vicarious liability:

Elements of Malpractice

- Respondeat Superior: Latin for *let the superior reply*. This doctrine is invoked when there is a master-servant relationship between two parties. The premise is that when an employer (master) is acting through the facility of an employee or agent (servant), and tort liability is incurred during the course of this agency because of some fault of the agent, then the employer (master) must accept the responsibility.
Eg: If a physician's office nurse injects medication into a patient's gluteus maximus and in the process hits the sciatic nerve and causes injury, the patient may sue the physician for the nurse's negligence.
- Captain of the Ship: This doctrine holds that a surgeon is liable based on the legal theory that he or she has absolute control much like the captain of a ship at sea who is responsible for all the wrongs perpetrated by the crew. This doctrine was intended to offer a remedy to a person injured by negligent employees of charitable hospitals which were otherwise legally immune from suit under the doctrine of charitable immunity.
- Borrowed Servant: This doctrine has largely replaced the captain of the ship doctrine. This doctrine holds surgeons responsible for hospital employees' negligence that is committed under their direct supervision and control.

Please keep the following concepts in mind when discussing issues of malpractice:

- To prevail in a medical malpractice action, the plaintiff must establish the proper standard of care and show a failure to comply with this standard was the proximate cause of the injury(ies) claimed.
- A bad result is not in and of itself proof of negligence. The plaintiff must show by affirmative evidence, usually espoused

by an expert witness, that the defendant was not properly skilled or was skilled yet performed in a negligent manner.
- An honest error of judgment, so long as that judgment was similar to that ordinarily exercised by qualified physicians in similar cases, is not necessarily negligence.
- If one of several forms of treatment were available, and the defendant chose one that later proved to not be the best choice, this is not negligence unless it is shown by the plaintiff to be considered inappropriate by the greater medical community at the time it was selected.

When assessing the physician's failure to meet the standard of care (the duty), an expert witness is utilized to establish that standard of care/duty. The expert witness does not merely say "I would not have done things that way," he/she must establish "No prudent/reasonable physician would have acted the way the defendant physician did." Thus the deviation cannot be something that just the expert would not perform, it must be one other physicians as a rule would not perform.

Note: the fact that a physician provided care that is *usual or customary* does not prevent the possibility of finding a breach of duty, as the usual and customary care might be found to be negligent.

Statute of Limitations

A statute of limitations is a law setting the time frame within which a legal action must be filed or after which a legal action may not be filed. In practical terms, each state has a statute of limitations identifying how long an individual has within which to initiate a malpractice lawsuit for a medical injury. That same statute of limitations will also set a deadline beyond which that lawsuit may not be initiated. The statute of limitations with regard to malpractice lawsuits will also stipulate within what time frame an individual must discover that an injury has in fact occurred.

The Locality Rule

What about the locality rule? The locality rule is an old, established concept that physicians are held to the standard of practice that is exhibited by other similarly situated physicians practicing in the same field. While Illinois still maintains some fealty to this rule, it is important to be cautious for a *minimal national standard* as today the Internet, telemedicine, national conferences, and national journals expose all physicians to the latest techniques of practice. However, remaining apprised of the practice techniques of colleagues in your community gives one a sense of what the community standard is. Anytime one practices within that standard, one is at least minimally protected from being considered as practicing outside the pale. It is certainly easier to find a colleague to support your practice, should it come into question, when the majority of those in your community are also practicing at the same standard. Note that while the locality rule still vestigially exists in Illinois, it has been greatly limited by the Illinois case of Purtill v Hess (111 Ill.2d229, 489 N.E.2d867 [1986]). In cases of informed consent issues, the locality rule has given way to *the reasonable physician standard* which is a national standard for reasonable and ordinary care. (Based upon the Illinois case of Hansbrough v Kosyak 141 Ill.App.3d538, 490N.E.2d181[1986])

CHAPTER 3

Informed Consent

LANDMARK CASES

1) *Natanson v Kline (Supreme Court of Kansas, 1960)*
2) *Canterbury v Spence (US Court of Appeals, District of Columbia, 1972)*
3) *Kaimowitz v Michigan Department of Mental Health (Michigan Circuit Court, Wayne County, 1973)*
4) *Truman v Thomas (Supreme Court of California, 1980)*
5) *Cruzan v Director, Missouri Department of Health (US Supreme Court, 1990)*

Informed consent is a central issue in the rendering of care to the patient. When offering medical care it is important for the patient to be aware of his/her options in treatment, the possible outcomes of accepting treatment and the possible outcomes of rejecting treatment. A decision is not valid if it is not informed. The cases that follow have set the tone for the concept of what a patient must know.

The concept of informed consent is inherent in its name, and yet it has evolved over time into its current concept. Inherent in the phrase is the meaning of the patient being informed about the medical treatment/procedure/medication and giving his/her consent for that.

1) ***Natanson v. Kline:*** This case dealt with Irma Natanson, who had a radical mastectomy in 1955 for breast cancer. After the surgery, Ms. Natanson turned to Dr. Kline, a radiologist for follow up radiation

Informed Consent

therapy. After the radiation therapy, Ms. Natanson's skin and muscles beneath her left arm sloughed away and the ribs of her left chest were so burned that they became necrotic. Ms. Natanson brought suit for malpractice claiming that 1) the radiation treatment had been performed in a negligent manner, and 2) she had not been informed of the risks. Dr. Kline testified that he knew there was a risk of injury however he "took a calculated risk." The Court reviewed the case and held the proper rule to determine whether the patient has given a valid consent to a proposed treatment compels the physician to assure that the physician has obtained an informed consent. The duty of the physician to disclose is limited to those disclosures which *a reasonable medical practitioner* would make under the same or similar circumstances. How the physician may best discharge his/her obligation to the patient in this difficult situation involves primarily a question of medical judgment. So long as the disclosure is sufficient to assure an informed consent, the physician's choice of plausible courses should not be called into question if it appears that the physician was motivated only by the patient's best therapeutic interests, and he/she proceeded as competent physicians would have done in a similar situation. The Court stated:

> *Each man is considered to be master of his own body and he may, if he be of sound mind, expressly prohibit the performance of even life saving surgery. A doctor might well believe that an operation is necessary, but the law does not permit him to substitute his own judgment for that of the patient by any form of deception. The physician should explain to the patient the nature of the ailment, the nature of the proposed treatment, the probability of success or of alternatives, and perhaps the risks of unfortunate results.*

This is a landmark case because it is the first court requirement of informed consent. This case set the standard for the *reasonable medical practitioner* standard of informed consent. The next case, Canterbury v Spence is contrasted in that it creates the standard of *materiality of the information.*

2) **Canterbury v. Spence**: In this case, Jerry Canterbury was a young man with back pain who worked as a clerk for the FBI. After not obtaining relief from the pain from two general practitioners, the patient, a 19 year old male, made an appointment with Dr. Spence, a neurosurgeon. Dr. Spence recommended that Jerry Canterbury undergo a laminectomy surgery to correct what Dr. Spence believed was a herniated disc. Since he was a minor, the patient's mother was given the information about the surgery and was told it was "no more dangerous than any other surgery." The patient later claimed he was not informed of the possibility in 1% of cases of resulting paraplegia. [Note, in this case the patient suffered paraplegia, yet it occurred not necessarily due to the surgery, it occurred instead due to a fall the patient experienced after the surgery while still in the hospital]. The Court found for the patient. It based its decision upon the following concepts:

Justice Cardozo in the 1914 case of Schloendorff v. Society of New York Hospital stated:

> *Every human being of adult years and sound mind has a right to determine what shall be done with his own body.*

The Court in the *Canterbury* case reasoned :

> *The patient's right of self-decision shapes the boundaries of the duty to reveal. That right can only be effectively exercised if the patient possesses sufficient information to enable an intelligent choice. The scope of the physician's communications to the patient, then, must be measured by the patient's need.*

This case outlined a new rule, that of *materiality of the information* standard. Unlike the *reasonable medical practitioner standard* espoused in the *Natanson* case, this standard relies on an objective, rather than a subjective test: What would a prudent person in the patient's position have decided if suitably informed of all perils bearing significance?

This case also describes exceptions to the requirement for informed consent:

- The first exception is when the patient is unconscious and harm from a failure to treat is imminent and outweighs any harm threatened by the proposed treatment. Although an attempt to secure a relative's consent is desirable, surgery should proceed without it if necessary.
- The therapeutic exception applies when risk disclosure poses such a threat of detriment to the patient as to become unfeasible or contraindicated. Patients on occasion become so distraught by disclosure that this stress precludes a rational decision or even poses the potential for psychological trauma. Disclosure to a close relative to secure consent may be the only alternative.

3) ***Kaimowitz v Michigan Department of Mental Health***: The issue raised in this case was whether an institutionalized mental patient could give informed consent for psychosurgery. In this case, Mr. Lewis Smith was committed to Ionia State Hospital in 1955 as a criminal sexual psychopath following a charge that he had murdered and then raped a student nurse while he was confined to a state mental hospital. In 1972, Mr. Smith was transferred to the Lafayette Clinic as a suitable subject for a research study on uncontrollable aggression. In this study, 24 criminal sexual psychopaths in the state mental health system were to be used in research to assess the effects of surgery on the limbic system of the brain versus the effects of an anti-androgenic hormone, to see which provided the greater

benefit in controlling aggression in males in an institutional setting. Smith had agreed in writing to allow himself to become an experimental subject. The plaintiff, Mr. Kaimowitz was an attorney who entered the case as Mr. Smith's advocate, and filed a suit to stop the study. The court considered the issue to be:

After failure of established therapies, may an adult or a legally appointed guardian, if the adult is involuntarily detained, give legally adequate consent to innovative or experimental surgical procedure on the brain.

The Court found that an institutionalized mental patient in this situation could NOT give informed consent because:

the very nature of his incarceration diminishes the capacity to consent to psychosurgery [thus making a truly free and voluntary decision impossible].

Thus the Court held that Mr. Smith's competency to give consent was impaired by:

- The mental condition of Mr. Smith
- The deprivation stemming from his involuntary confinement
- The effects of the phenomena of institutionalization

The Court further noted that an involuntarily detained mental patient was in an inherently coercive atmosphere, unable to give true informed consent for psychosurgery.

The Court stated:

A person involuntarily detained in a state facility cannot give legally adequate consent to an innovative or experimental surgical procedure on the brain where the danger

Informed Consent

is high and the risks incapable of assessment. [If the surgery were widely accepted in the field, such as for a brain tumor, the court would be willing to accept the consent]

The rest of the story: The Michigan Department of Mental Health did NOT challenge the standing of Mr. Kaimowitz because it wanted a ruling on this issue.

4) ***Truman v Thomas***: In this case the children of Rena Truman sued her doctor, Dr. Claude Thomas, a family practitioner, for the wrongful death of their mother. Rena Truman had been under Dr. Thomas' care from 1963 until March 1969. During that time, Dr. Thomas had not performed a Pap smear for Mrs. Truman. Dr. Thomas indicated that he had suggested a Pap test on several occasions to Mrs. Truman, however she had declined the test due to concerns about cost and for other unspecified reasons. Dr. Thomas noted that the use and reasons for the Pap test were widely understood by the public and that he felt that his patient had a high degree of responsibility. He felt he was an advisor. It is noted that the patient deceased from cervical cancer.

The Court held that the doctor's duty was to make available all material information to assist the patient in her decision-making process:

Material information is that which the physician knows would be regarded as significant by a reasonable person in the patient's position when deciding to accept or reject a recommended medical procedure. To be material, a fact must also be one which is not commonly appreciated.

If a patient indicates that he or she is going to decline a test or treatment, then the doctor has the additional duty of advising of the material risks of which a reasonable person would want to be informed before deciding not to undergo the procedure.

NOTE: This case can be viewed as an extension of the <u>Canterbury</u> case in that the physician must not only explain the risks and benefits of accepting a medical procedure, he/she must also explain the risks and benefits of declining a procedure.

5) ***Cruzan v Director, Missouri Department of Health***: On January 11, 1983, Nancy Cruzan lost control of her car and suffered a severe motor vehicle accident. She was discovered without any detectable respiratory or cardiac function. She had been without oxygen for at least 12 to 14 minutes before paramedics were able to resuscitate her. Ms. Cruzan received food/nutrition and liquid via a gastrostomy tube. Ms. Cruzan existed in a persistent vegetative state without signs of significant cognitive functioning for six years. Ms. Cruzan's parents requested that her artificial nutrition and hydration support be terminated. Hospital employees refused to honor this request. A state court authorized the termination, finding that Nancy Cruzan had a right under the state and federal constitutions to order withdrawal of death-prolonging procedures. The court construed Nancy Cruzan's verbal expression to a former house mate that she would not want to continue her life should she ever become a "vegetable" [purported to be Nancy Cruzan's own words] to mean that she would not wish to continue receiving nutrition and hydration through artificial means. The Missouri Supreme Court reversed the finding of the state court. The Missouri Supreme Court refused to read into the state constitution a broad right to privacy that would support an unrestricted right to refuse treatment. The Missouri Supreme Court held that Nancy Cruzan's statements made to her house mate were unreliable for the purpose of determining her intent with regard to life and death. The issue in this case: did Nancy Cruzan have a right under the US Constitution to direct the withdrawal of life-sustaining treatment, and if so, whether a state may require clear and convincing evidence to support an incompetent's wishes as to the withdrawal of life-sustaining treatment.

Informed Consent

Judge Rehnquist, writing for the United States Supreme Court in a 5-4 majority vote, concluded that the US Constitution does NOT forbid the state of Missouri from requiring that the proof required to establish an incompetent's wishes for the withdrawal of life-sustaining treatment be supported by clear and convincing evidence.

Note that the question put to the US Supreme Court was simply whether the US Constitution prohibited Missouri from choosing the decision of requiring clear and convincing evidence. This is the first case in which the US Supreme Court was presented with whether the US Constitution grants *a right to die*. The 14th Amendment provides a constitutionally protected liberty interest in refusing unwanted medical treatment in a competent person. However, whether a person's constitutional rights have been violated must be determined by balancing his/her liberty interests against relevant state interests. The Court stated that it assumed that the US Constitution would grant a competent person a constitutionally protected right to refuse life saving nutrition and hydration. An incompetent person is not able to make an informed and voluntary choice to exercise a hypothetical right to refuse treatment.

Key Issues in Consent

Remember to obtain consent. Do NOT rely on the concept of *implied consent* [consent that is found to exist solely because certain actions or signs would lead a reasonable person to believe that the consent is present, whether or not that consent is even specifically expressed]. Implied consent may be present in an emergency situation wherein the patient is incapable of giving consent due to the loss of consciousness, due to the need for immediate reaction without time to explain the situation and necessary interventional procedure(s), due to the inability to access family or appropriate guardian in the face of immediately needed medical response. Other than in an emergency situation, be certain to obtain consent. The issue of competency comes in to play when obtaining consent, as informed consent is neither informed nor consensual if the individual lacks the requisite cognitive skills to appreciate the situation, to appreciate the options, to appreciate the risks, to appreciate the potential benefit, to communicate an answer.

Adhere to the scope of consent. Keep in mind that when a patient gives permission for you as the physician to proceed with a medical therapy, with an interventional procedure, a surgical operation, with the prescribing of medication, the patient is understanding certain parameters for the treatment: the scope of the treatment. The scope of the consent is limited to whatever parameters were expressed before the medical intervention [in an emergency situation the extension of that scope may be implied]. As a general rule, a physician commits a battery if he/she exceeds the limits of the permission [consent] given by the patient. What is the reason? Because the consent is neither informed nor consensual: the patient was neither aware of the components necessary to understand what has happened [the informed component], nor has the patient been offered the opportunity to say yay or nay [the consensual component]. Example: a physician who performed a non-emergent hysterectomy when he found infected fallopian tubes during surgery on a patient who had consented only to a repair of a lacerated uterus was held liable [*King v Carney*, 204P.270 (1922)]. If the patient gives permission to the physician to remedy a condition rather than to perform a specific procedure, the courts will usually allow the physician to render treatments reasonably necessary to correct the condition.

The whole nine yards. In obtaining informed consent, be sure the following nine elements have been addressed:

- Inform the patient of his/her condition
- Inform the patient of his/her presumptive diagnosis
- Inform the patient of his/her potential differential diagnoses
- Inform the patient of any and all diagnostic/treatment tests (and once performed, of the results)

Informed Consent

- Inform the patient of all treatment options
- Inform the patient of associated risks
- Inform the patient of any alternative options (the possibility of other non-traditional treatment approaches): failure to explain an alternative treatment to a patient might constitute negligence. If other treatment options exist, and if the physician is not comfortable with these options, if these options are part of the current medical arena, the physician is best advised to discuss the option(s) and allow the patient to seek further counsel from those better trained in such option(s). While some of the other options may seem somewhat on the fringe, it may still be prudent to mention these options and explain their novel patina while giving the patient the opportunity to peruse those options on his/her own.
- Inform the patient of his/her prognosis
- Inform the patient of your expectations as a physician without giving any warranties

Obtaining Informed Consent

Now comes the question "Who obtains the informed consent from the patient?" Does the office manager, does the office nurse, can the resident in training, can the medical student? Courts are eminently clear in their written opinions that the responsibility to obtain informed consent from a patient clearly remains with the physician, and this responsibility canNOT be delegated. While it is common practice for others to obtain the signature on a form, the reality is that it is the responsibility, the duty, of the physician to explain the procedure, the medication, the risks, the side effects, the hoped for benefits to the patient. And what about consent forms?

Consent Forms

Does a signed consent form serve as a shield against a malpractice action or as a shield against the patient claiming he/she did not understand the procedure, risks, dangers? Absolutely not! The signed form may serve as evidence that the patient was informed of something or that an attempt was made to give information, however it is NOT determinative. Adequate informed consent is best established by an accurate narrative documentation written by the attending physician. When a patient alleges that a physician failed to obtain valid consent to treatment, the primary question likely to be asked is: "What did the physician tell the patient?" Remember that most professional negligence actions (malpractice actions) do not come to the courtroom until at least two to three years have passed; thus it is important to document the information communicated to the patient concerning any proposed treatment at the time you are presenting it to the patient.

Keep in mind that if a physician obtains informed consent from a patient for the performance of a surgical procedure, and another physician actually performs the procedure, the patient may sue the operating surgeon for battery or for malpractice (based upon the theory of no informed consent) as the patient had consented to the surgery being performed by Surgeon A and not by Surgeon B.

A recap: informed consent is based upon three main ingredients –

- Knowledge: being given adequate information to make an educated decision
- Voluntariness: the patient, based upon the information given, must voluntarily proceed
- Competence: the patient must be competent (intellectually/cognitively capable) of understanding the issues at hand, to voluntarily give consent, and able to communicate this)

Exceptions to the need for material disclosure

Disclosing of material and relevant information is based upon the concept of a material risk that is a particular inherent risk that a

Informed Consent

physician knows or ought to know would be a significant factor in a reasonable person's decision whether to reject or accept treatment. Thus the scope of disclosure of inherent risks that are material, must be measured by the patient's need to know whether a potential peril is material in making an intelligent informed choice. There are four generally recognized exceptions to the physician's duty to make prior disclosure of material risks, although all four might not necessarily be available in a particular state:

- *Therapeutic privilege/professional discretion:* in his or her professional judgment a physician may conclude that disclosure of a risk poses such a threat or detriment to the patient that it is contraindicated from a medical point of view. Withholding the information is not based upon the physician's belief that a patient would probably refuse treatment if informed of the material risks, it must be based upon the physician's belief that disclosure would be harmful, dangerous, or injurious to the patient. Withholding information must be based on the physician's established knowledge that his/her patient will be unduly alarmed by a full disclosure.
- *The competent patient who seeks not to know:* A physician need not disclose the nature and risks of a treatment to a patient who specifically requests that he/she not be told. The patient may reject disclosure out of a desire to remain ignorant, or the patient may have already had a similar medical experience.
- *Common Knowledge:* A physician is privileged not to advise the patient of matters that are common knowledge or of which the patient has actual knowledge, particularly on the basis of past experience.
- *Emergency Situation:* no duty to inform arises in an emergency in which the patient is unconscious or otherwise incapable of giving valid consent and harm from failure to treat is imminent and outweighs any harm threatened by the proposed treatment.

Informed Consent Causes of Action

[A claim in law and fact sufficient to form the basis of a valid lawsuit]

An action based upon failure to provide informed consent is based upon one or any combination of the following four concepts:

- Assault and Battery
- Negligence involving the [failure of the] duty to disclose
- The tort of lack of informed consent
- The ethical and legal respect for dignity, autonomy, and life

Defenses to a Cause of Action for a Lack of Informed Consent

As a physician, the following defenses are available on the part of your attorney to protect you from a successful lawsuit in a cause of action for failure to obtain informed consent:

- Documentation in your chart demonstrating a session with the patient wherein you gave the requisite information and obtained the patient's consent.
- The lack of immediate capacity for the person to consent. Eg: emergency situation.
- The *so what* defense: When asserting this defense the court will give the physician an opportunity to contend that even if his or her patient had been informed of the risk at issue, the patient would have consented to the treatment.
- The *unduly alarming* defense provides the defendant physician with an opportunity to contend that material information was withheld because he/she was acting in the patient's best interest. [Therapeutic Privilege]

In reviewing the landmark cases, and in applying them to the concept of informed consent when discussing medical intervention with your patients, I recommend the following approach as a guide:

Informed Consent

- First, ascertain any pertinent legal mandates in your jurisdiction with regard to informed consent.
- Second, explain to your patient, in very clear terms, in very clear and understandable language, not using medical jargon, not using medical *babble* or *psychobabble* :
  1) what your diagnosis is for the patient
  2) what that means for therapeutic prognosis
  3) what the possible approaches are
  4) what the medicational/procedural approaches are
  5) what the risks, side-effects, and benefits of the medication(s)/procedure(s) are
  6) what the risks are of not treating with medication(s)/procedure(s)
- Third, ask the patient his/her understanding of what you have just explained and have him/her explain it in his/her own words (chart this also).
- Fourth, with the patient's permission, explain all of the above to family members if they can be present and ascertain their understanding of the stated material.
- Fifth, if the patient is either a minor or incompetent, be certain that the appropriate guardian has been informed of all of the above, expresses understanding of all of the above.
- Sixth, have the patient/guardian sign a form acknowledging that you have explained the foregoing and he/she has affixed his/her signature to signify both understanding and to give informed consent for the initiation of the medication (or the performance of the procedure).

Recommendation – chart every time you initiate a medication the following statement:

> *I discussed with the patient the risks and side-effects of the medication, [name of medication(s)], as well as its potential benefits, and discussed the following risks and*

side-effects, including and not limited to: [example of an antipsychotic – dystonic reaction, Parkinsonian-like tremor, long term muscle movement disturbance known as tardive dyskinesia, neuroleptic malignant syndrome in which one out of five sufferers may die, akathisia and metabolic syndrome]. Patient expressed understanding of the information, and in his/her own words described appropriately all that I had discussed and gave informed consent for initiation of the [name of medication(s)] at [give initial dose] with upward titration as clinically indicated.

I also recommend demonstrating visually the possible side-effects if they lend themselves to a visual demonstration. If you have printed hand-outs for each of the medications that you might prescribe, (or procedures you perform) that is also something to give to patients and document in the chart that the patient received the informational hand-out.

Again, I cannot emphasize enough that your explanations must be in plain, clear language. If your patient is not fluent in English, be sure that someone versed in the patient's native tongue is able to translate clearly to the patient what you have explained and have the patient repeat back to his/her interpreter his/her understanding of what was said to him/her so that you can verify his/her clear understanding.

Explain to patient that if certain side-effects are life-threatening, should the side-effects manifest, that he/she should go immediately to the nearest emergency room at the hospital and have you paged from there.

Remember also, that if the patient refuses the medication or procedure, to explain to the patient the prognosis for the condition if medication is not used, or procedure is not undertaken. Also, discuss

Informed Consent

alternative therapeutic approaches, noting that you might not be the appropriate practitioner for providing those services, yet that they are also options to consider.

Duty to Disclose - How Much Is Enough?

You might ask: How much duty to disclose do I as the physician have? Do I have to list each and every possible risk and side effect listed in the PDR? The Court in *Miceikis v Field* addressed this issue (37 Ill.App.3d 763, 347 N.E.2d 320 [1st District 1976]):

> *Green imposed the limitation of foreseeable risks, but did not comment on materiality. In our view, it would be too onerous a burden to place upon a physician the duty of disclosing every conceivable risk which possibly could develop. As the expert testimony revealed in the present case, excessive disclosure of remote risks would tend to do more harm than good to the patient. A doctor has a special relationship with his patient...This relationship not only vests the doctor with the responsibility of disclosure, but also requires the doctor to exercise discretion in prudently disclosing information in accordance with his patient's best interests. To disclose more than that which is material would run counter to the responsibility assumed through the doctor-patient relationship... This standard of disclosure, as established through expert medical testimony, would define the doctor's duty as informing of those factors, either alone or in combination with other factors, which the patient would view as significant enough to influence this decision of whether or not to consent to therapy [found at page 324, 347 N.E.2d].*

Note that the standard of disclosure is a question of proof at trial and ultimately relies upon the testimony of expert witnesses. When a difference of opinion exists between expert witnesses (as is apt to be the case in a malpractice suit based upon informed consent) the question becomes one for the trier of fact.

In Illinois, in cases where plaintiffs argue that had they been adequately informed they would not have undergone a given procedure (or initiated a given medication), the standard used to determine the appropriate informed consent is the Objective Standard: what would a reasonable person have decided if given adequate information (disclosure) about the procedure/medication. The idea is to protect the defendant physician from the 20/20 hindsight of a disgruntled plaintiff dissatisfied with the outcome. Guess what? Often this again results in dueling experts giving opinions that are ultimately resolved by the jury.

CHAPTER 4

Medical Records

Let us look at medical records and some of the important issues that surround them. Medical records are important from a practice perspective in that they contain the information about each and every patient we see. They give us the information we need each time we see a patient; they serve as our peripheral brain to remember what has happened for and with this patient since we established the patient/physician relationship. The record is also important should we have another physician covering for us and he/she is able to understand our patient from the data we have placed into our medical record. What is important at this point:

- Write legibly [when using hand written notes/charts as opposed to Electronic Medical Records].
- Include data that is pertinent to this patient's care.
- Avoid subjective editorial comments.
- Include your thoughts on diagnoses and possible future paths if current treatments are not effective: giving your thoughtful treatment "algorithm" will help other physicians who may either be covering for you or who assume your patient's care should the patient change physicians for whatever reason.
- Document communications with the patient, including and not limited to informed consent for all treatment approaches.

Keep in mind that a medical record might become part of a legal proceeding. Statistics demonstrate that medical evidence is estimated to play a part in about three quarters of all civil cases and in about one quarter of criminal cases brought to trial [Matte, *Legal Implications of the Patient's Medical Record*, in *Legal Medicine Annual*: 1971, 345-375 (C.H. Wecht ed., 1971)].

So what does this mean? Well, it means that your medical record can serve as

- A means of maintaining continuity of care
- A legal document used as evidence in the courtroom

Given the above, it means that this document should be properly kept: updated appropriately, neat and legible, free from inappropriate subjective musings. The medical record must be accurate and should not be tampered with. If an error is made, how do you deal with it? For handwritten medical records/charts/notes:

- First, never erase an error (these look suspicious).
- Never obliterate an error (again, this may create suspicion).
- The appropriate method is to draw one simple line through the error. Initial the line, date it and identify it with the word "error." Then write the correct entry.

For electronic medical records/electronic health records:

- Add an addendum that is properly dated and explain what was meant in the first note. Properly date and electronically sign the addendum.

From a medicolegal perspective, alterations to records can prove disastrous. Records with obvious alterations, particularly any record that can be shown to have been "doctored" can prove deadly in court. Tampering with medical records may result in large malpractice awards even when there has been no negligence. Do not add, delete, substitute or remove. If anything is added, it must be properly notated, dated, and signed.

Remember that falsification of a medical record to conceal negligence or a criminal violation may be found civilly and/or criminally actionable. In Michigan, for example, it is a crime to deliberately falsify a medical record [Mich.Stat.Ann. §14.624(21)(Callaghan 1976)]. Also remember that if you have improperly altered a medical record and it becomes part of a legal proceeding via a subpoena, you may be subject to criminal prosecution. Keep in mind that document examination has become a sophisticated science and the ability to actually tell the time entries were made has become very exact.

Please be careful in using abbreviations in the medical record. The abbreviation in Psychiatry of TCA means a tricyclic antidepressant; however, in Dermatology it means trichloroacetic acid and has a completely different use. To avoid ambiguity and future treatment error or record misinterpretation, please avoid abbreviations wherever and whenever possible.

MEDICAL RECORDS AND PRIVACY AND CONFIDENTIALITY

As a rule of thumb, as a physician you have a fiduciary duty (the highest degree of legal obligation or duty) to protect a patient's privacy/confidentiality. The patient's right to privacy is based upon legal doctrines found in the 9th Amendment to the US Constitution via the penumbral rights. The Federal Privacy Act also recognizes this right to privacy. This statute requires federal agencies to obtain the consent of individuals before the disclosure of any record kept by a government agency, including medical records, unless it is for the census or for civil or criminal prosecution. Communication between the physician and the patient held to be confidential includes all data that the physician has found by directly examining the patient, objectively studying the patient through laboratory tests, x rays, scans, electrical conduction studies. Unless the patient has given permission to release this information, it may not be released even to family members (if the patient is over the age of majority).

Who owns the medical record and who can have access to it? The courts and legislatures recognize two types of ownership:

- The physical record
- The information contained in the record

The physician owns the actual record, the patient owns the information contained in the record. Under HIPAA, patients are entitled access to their medical records. Keep in mind that mental health records may not be released if disclosure of the information contained therein could endanger the patient's welfare. My rule of thumb is to chart in my record with the thought at all times that this record may be read by another physician or clinician, and may be read at any time by the patient him or herself. That serves as a reminder in maintaining accurate, nonjudgmental documentation, with clear thoughts as to treatment direction and planning. While a patient ultimately has a right to either see his/her record or to secure a copy of his/her record, the request must be reasonable. If you as a physician deem it appropriate to allow the patient access to his record, the event should be supervised and monitored. As a physician, you should make yourself available when the patient wishes to review the records. Remember that if you refuse the patient access to his/her record, he/she may obtain a court order. What is the reason you supervise the process? Because you want to be certain the patient neither adds nor removes parts of his/her record; you want to be certain the patient makes no changes in his/her record. The patient may add an addendum that states it is written by the patient and gives the date and time.

How long should you retain medical records? This is in part determined by statute in the state in which you practice. It is either dictated by a specific medical record retention statute or by the time limitations (statute of limitations) created via the malpractice statutes. By determining the time frame in which a legal action

Medical Records

may be brought for medical malpractice, this will dictate the minimum of how long you should retain records. It is beneficial to retain a patient's medical records indefinitely for so long as the patient is alive and you are in practice. When you retire, it is prudent to maintain the records in a safe storage area with the likelihood that the patient will request the record (a copy thereof) be sent to the new treating physician for purposes of continuity of care.

CHAPTER 5

The Physician-Patient Relationship

Unless and until a physician-patient relationship has been established, you as a physician are not legally compelled to treat strangers, even during an emergency, in almost all states. When a person seeks the services of a physician for the purposes of medical or surgical treatment, that person becomes a patient and a traditional physician-patient relationship is created. A contract is implied by the mutuality of the relationship. Creation of this relationship usually requires some form of physical contact with the patient. It may be created by a single telephone conversation. The courts tend to be very generous in assessing the creation of the physician-patient relationship. What courts will look to is did the patient have a reasonable expectation of treatment and/or did the physician undertake to render treatment. As stated in the case of *Kirschner v. Equitable Life Assurance Soc.*, 248 N.Y.S. 506 (1935):

> *the broad term covering all steps taken to effect a cure of an injury or disease. The word includes examination and diagnosis as well as application of remedies* [in defining the word treatment]

This broad interpretation and the willingness of most courts to find a relationship to exist based upon the patient's reliance and expectations, may result in the finding of a physician-patient relationship that the physician never intended to create.

The Physician-Patient Relationship

Keep in mind that once the physician-patient relationship has been created, unless you limit it or condition it via agreement with the patient (put it in writing and have both of your signatures affixed and witnessed and dated), it continues until you and the patient terminate the relationship. Once the relationship has been terminated, you as the physician are generally not obligated to follow the patient's progress. Note that if you and the patient feel that the patient no longer needs your services and you both agree that the relationship is terminated, it is prudent in today's environment to send the patient a letter noting that your services are no longer required and the relationship is being terminated at this time. Place a copy of the letter in the patient's chart. Please keep in mind that this must be done with the understanding of the patient so as to avoid the issue of abandonment. Remember, abandonment is the act of discontinuing care to a patient who is still in need of care. It is actionable as a malpractice action. We discuss that in the malpractice section.

When establishing a physician/patient relationship explain to the patient what limits you may need to place on your availability. If this is an issue for the patient it needs to be clearly spelled out and may require you to refer the patient elsewhere.

Note that physicians are generally free to choose their patients and are not obligated to treat anyone with whom they have no special relationship. Absent a statute imposing a requirement to treat, physicians are not compelled to practice, to practice under terms other than those the physician may choose to accept, or to provide care to any or all prospective patients. Keep in mind that once you have established a relationship with a patient as his/her physician you assume the duty to exercise the same degree of knowledge, skill, diligence, and care that any ordinary competent physician would exercise under the same or similar circumstances. This carries with it the implied duty to suggest a referral if you know (or should have known) that you do not possess the requisite knowledge or skill to properly treat the patient. Thus, failure to make a referral in the instance of areas outside of your expertise, is negligence.

Physicians are under no obligation to give gratuitous advice. However, once advice is given, even casual free advice at a party, a duty arises of due care to anyone who might reasonably rely on that advice. If the gratuitous advice causes injury, one may be liable for the injury. If one relies upon advice, even advice given gratuitously, to his or her own detriment, then the concept of *detrimental reliance* may cause liability to arise and attach. The degree of contact may be determinative.

CHAPTER 6

Medical Malpractice Insurance

Insurance in essence is a form of gambling. You, the physician, are hoping that during your practice lifetime you will not have a lawsuit brought against you for your practice of medicine. However, you will hedge your bets by purchasing a malpractice insurance policy. The company that sells you the policy is also hoping you never face a lawsuit. In fact, not only are they hoping you don't, they are actually gambling that you won't. They accept from you a small fee each year (a premium) to provide you protection (coverage) should you find yourself in litigation for malpractice. In order to improve their odds, the insurance company spreads the risk by creating a large pool of subscribers who all pay into the fund. The insurance company tries to improve the odds even more by writing a contract very carefully that excludes certain losses. The concept of the insurance contract is to define very specifically the losses that are covered and those that are not. As a result, certain conditions, limitations, and exceptions are used to limit the insurance company's liability. Because the performance of the insurance contract depends on an event that may or may not occur, the insurance contract is called an *aleatory contract*. Insurance contracts are also known as *adhesion contracts* [a contract so heavily restrictive of one party, while so nonrestrictive of another, that doubts arise as to whether it is a voluntary agreement. The term signifies a grave inequality of bargaining power that may lead the contract to be declared invalid. The concept often arises in standard-form printed contracts submitted by one party to the other on a take-it-or-leave-it basis].

It is interesting to note that in our society no written contract is more prevalent than the insurance contract and probably no contract is less read by the purchaser. The purchaser (that means YOU) typically begins to read the contract only after a loss has occurred and then only to determine if indeed that loss is covered by the policy (contract).

Instead of belaboring the law of insurance, I am going to cut directly to the chase of what is really important to you as a physician in purchasing malpractice insurance. You need to determine whether to buy an occurrence policy or a claims-made policy. And you need to know what a tail is.

OCCURRENCE POLICY

These policies cover incidents that occur during the policy period without regard to when the claims are reported. The policy that is in effect at the time a service is performed covers any and all claims based on that service that may be reported in the future.

CLAIMS-MADE POLICY

These policies cover claims reported during the policy period regardless of when the service was rendered [with some exceptions]. Thus claims reported this year are covered by this year's policy and claims reported next year are covered by next year's policy.

So what does this all mean? How do you know which policy to purchase? If a policy is maintained with the same insurance company throughout your entire practice lifetime, there is little difference in actual coverage between the occurrence policy and most claims-made policies. However, remember they are different products with different benefits and advantages. The cost of these policy types is different.

Keep in mind that the average medical malpractice claim is made several years after the incident. Add to that the time for investigation and

Medical Malpractice Insurance

either court time or settlement. If a full trial occurs with a jury it could be many years from the incident to the resolution. Thus, it is important to be with an insurance company that is financially sound and will be around a long time. Needless to say, an occurrence policy covers all future claims regardless of when reported; the company must still be in existence to pay the claim. The claims-made policy covers a claim for an act or omission filed during the time the policy is in effect.

Insurance companies may require the following:

- The insured (YOU, the physician) has no prior knowledge of the claim at the time the policy went into effect [you are not hiding something that happened or withholding information from your insurer].
- A retroactive exclusion limits claims covered to those that occur during the policy period or after a retroactive date (normally the date of the first claims-made policy with that company).
- Prior coverage of the claim for incidents occurring before the commencement of the policy is required, sometimes with the same company.

What can result? Let us look at the case of *Gereboff v Home Indemnity Company* [Gereboff v Home Indemnity Co. 383A.2d 1024 (R.I. 1978)]. The case involved an accounting firm. This firm had 3 continuous malpractice insurance policies, each with a different company:

DATE	EVENT	INSURER
1968	Incident Occurred	Home Indemnity Policy
1971	Malpractice Discovered	St. Paul Fire and Marine
1973	Lawsuit Filed	American Home Indemnity Co.

What happened? First of all, Home Indemnity Insurance did NOT cover the malpractice because the claim was not reported during its policy period. St. Paul did NOT cover because no claim was made during its policy coverage. American Home Indemnity did NOT cover because it had an exclusion clause for acts that occurred before the retroactive date when its first policy was written. Thus Gereboff was OOL: out of luck. As this case illustrates, gaps in coverage can occur in claims-made policies. Gaps do NOT occur when changing from an occurrence policy to a claims-made policy, however, gaps can occur when switching from one claims-made policy carrier to another or when the insured ceases to purchase claims-made policies. Thus, if a claims-made policy is ended, the insured (that means YOU) has no coverage for claims arising from incidents before the termination date and reported after that date. By the same token, the new insurance carrier would not provide coverage because of the prior act's exclusion.

How do you remedy this dilemma? You *purchase your tail* or in more technical jargon: you purchase *a reporting endorsement* to the policy. The *tail* or *reporting endorsement* is an amendment to the insurance policy that provides that all claims arising from actions that occurred during the term of prior claims-made policies are covered regardless of when they are reported. In essence the amendment puts these claims on the occurrence basis.

CHAPTER 7

Issues in Risk Management

What is Risk Management? Risk management, by its definition, is the careful control of situations, practices, activities that are fraught with potential adverse outcomes. In the learning and practice of medicine there are constant inherent risks of misdiagnosis, not performing a procedure correctly, mis-prescribing medication, adverse responses to medication, misadventures in surgery – the list is very long. The real key in medicine more than risk management is risk skill development. It is important to develop the skills to both avoid the adverse outcomes that are possible and to manage those outcomes if they do occur. How do we avoid those adverse outcomes and manage them should they occur? By paying close attention to the following areas:

- Communication
- Obtaining Informed Consent
- Appropriate Charting/Record Keeping

It is also important for us to have a good understanding of three other important areas:

- Malpractice
- Malpractice Insurance
- HIPAA

COMMUNICATION

Communication is the transfer of information from one person to another. It usually takes the form of conversation. However it may appear in written or other nonverbal forms. For physicians (whether attending, fellow, resident, intern, or medical student) the communication is important in transferring and obtaining information to and from:

- Colleagues
- Nursing Staff
- Technicians
- Laboratory Staff
- Nurse Practitioners
- Physician Assistants
- The Patient
- The Patient's Family

As physicians we communicate by speech, physical action, written orders, and chart notations. It is important that our communications are clear, understandable, and what we truly intend to convey. Short, terse, cold statements can be misinterpreted by patients as uncaring and unfeeling. Short, terse, cold statements can also be misinterpreted as disinterest. Non-empathic communications to patients can exacerbate patient dissatisfaction with a procedural outcome, leading to a possible malpractice action. At the least, warm, empathic responses can allow a patient to feel more "cared for" and enhance the healing process. At the most, warm empathic responses can avoid a misunderstanding and avert an unnecessary malpractice suit. Physical actions speak louder than words – the physician who stands at the door to the patient's room, with his/her hand on the doorknob, and talks to the patient for 30 minutes, will be perceived as less attentive and caring than the physician who is seated in the patient's room and talks with the patient for only 5 minutes. The patient will perceive the seated physician as truly interested based upon the body language, not based upon the time involved.

Communication with nursing staff, nurse practitioners, physician assistants, technicians, and laboratory staff is critical. These are the members of the medical team that perform the orders we write, that care for the patient when we are not there, that give us the information we need to assess the patient's physical status. It is important for us to realize that we are part of a team; how we treat the rest of that team will impact the treatment of the patient. It is important to keep in mind that we cannot be everywhere at once, we cannot know all there is to know, and we sometimes overlook pieces of information that are vital to our patients' care. If we create and maintain an open network of communication with our colleagues and ancillary staff members, we are more likely to receive important information from them. And keep in mind that ancillary staff also chart. We do not want others to chart based upon an unconscious resentment of us due to our communicated relationship to and with them.

When we write orders, it is important that our orders be clear in their meaning so that there is neither ambiguity nor confusion. It is also imperative that our orders be written legibly. If our orders cannot be read, they cannot be performed. If they are written illegibly, they may be performed in error and the liability will inure to us. If we maintain friendly, yet professional open channels of communication with all staff, they will feel comfortable asking us for clarifications in our orders if questions exist. If we communicate in a tyrannical fashion, staff will hesitate to question an order that may have been written in error, thus jeopardizing the safety of the patient and undermining our own treatment plan.

Keep in mind as well, that colleagues and staff are not mind readers. We cannot expect them to know what our treatment plan is if we have not communicated with them clearly and completely. Failure to do this may lead to errors in patient care when we are not readily available and split-second decisions need to be made by staff with regard to patients under our care.

And what about communication directly to and with the patient? This is of utmost importance. It is important that we communicate clearly from the onset of treatment with our patients. It is important that we begin the process in a warm manner, putting the patient at ease. Keep in mind that patients come to the physician, office, hospital, emergency room in a time of need; they do not know what is wrong with them and are coming as supplicants seeking help. Most often they are frightened. It is important that we help to calm the patient and family so that they are able to:

- Understand our question(s) without being anxious
- Communicate to us their symptoms
- Communicate to us their history
- Understand our provisional diagnosis
- Understand our recommended interventions
- Understand our recommended treatment approach
- Provide permission to proceed

Remember, in communicating with the patient and the patient's family, do so IN CLEAR LANGUAGE. It is a moment of pride for YOUR family to know you are in medical school and to hear you speak in complicated, long medical terms. It is a moment of confusion and angst for patients and THEIR families to hear you speak in the same *medicalese*. Keep in mind, there is nothing so complex that cannot be made simple and understandable. Remember that most patients and most patients' families have NOT attended medical school. They do not own a medical dictionary. And, they are under stress during the time. Thus, please speak to them in terms of plain, clear, and unambiguous language that they can understand. If English is not their first language, please be sure that you have someone available to translate what you are saying and asking into the patient/family's native language. It is also important that in speaking with families and patients that you perform a very important task: obtaining informed consent.

INFORMED CONSENT (refer to Chapter 3)

Just as Newton's third law of motion states that "for every action there is an equal and opposite reaction," extrapolated to medicine it implies that for every medical intervention there is the equal and opposite potential for risks and side-effects. The two key issues that present are:

1) What to tell the patient with regard to the risks, side-effects, and benefits of the proposed medical intervention
and
2) What to expect if the patient has an adverse response

CHAPTER 8

HIPAA: To Be or Not to Be (included)

First one must ask, "What is HIPAA?" Enacted by the United States Congress in 1996, it is officially the Health Insurance Portability and Accountability Act. It is purported to protect patients from abuse and fraud, and its purpose was to provide portability of health insurance when employees change from job to job. Part of its purported purpose was to create standards for privacy and confidentiality. It also is touted as curtailing costs by providing for electronic billing to consolidate expenses. Let us look at the act from a de minimis perspective to understand what is required for one to be included or excluded from the mandate of being a "covered provider."

1) As a physician, you are mandated to participate in HIPAA (that means to become HIPAA compliant) if and only if you electronically send or receive one or more of 11 specified transactions. These 11 transactions are covered by HIPAA. If you can say yes to any one or more of the following, you are HIPAA mandated. If you can say with gusto, "*I do none of the below,*" then you are HIPAA exempted:

    a) You transmit or receive electronically either Health care claims or an equivalent type of encounter information and/or
    b) You send or receive health care payment information or payment service advice and/or
    c) You participate electronically in the coordination of benefits and/or

HIPAA: To Be or Not to Be (included)

d) You either send or receive information electronically with regard to the status of a health care claim and/or
e) You participate in the enrollment or disengagement into or out of health care plans via electronic transmission and/or
f) You determine patient eligibility for a given health care plan via electronic transmission and/or
g) You send or receive health plan premium payments/payment information via electronic means and/or
h) You send or receive certification and/or authorization for patients to be seen in your practice via electronic means and/or
i) You send or receive the first report of injury via electronic means and/or
j) You send or receive health claims attachments via electronic means and/or
k) You participate electronically in other transactions as designated by regulation by the Secretary of Health and Human Services

NOTE: the key to all of the above is the transmission or receipt of information electronically with regard to the treatment of patients (their treatment, billing, insurance company participation).

2) If you do business with any company representing you and they are engaged in the practice of transmitting and receiving information with regard to your patients' treatment, or insurance participation or eligibility for treatment, electronically, you might then be subsumed under the rules and regulations of being a HIPAA mandated provider, even if your office itself does not.

To paraphrase Mica 6:8 *What does the Lord require of thee O man, to love mercy, to do justice, and to walk humbly with thy G-D*, to avoid HIPAA what is required of thee O physician, to bill the old fashioned way, to maintain fewer than 10 full time equivalent employees, and to disengage your fax machine so as not to receive or send any patient information with regard to billing, eligibility, health claims, coordination of benefits, referrals, or injury reports.

What about privacy and confidentiality, you ask? Even if you are not required to participate in HIPAA per se, the privacy rule as stipulated under HIPAA has become the national minimum standard for confidentiality and protection of patient records/information. Thus it is important to familiarize yourself with that provision and to maintain a standard of care for confidentiality and privacy that comports with that component of the HIPAA act.

CHAPTER 9

Guidelines for Courtroom Testimony

It is important to keep in mind that during your practice as a physician you may be called upon to appear in a Court of Law for different reasons:

- You may be called as a witness
- You may present as a plaintiff
- You may present as a defendant
- You may present in a deposition
- You may be called upon to bring information/records to the court

If called as a witness, it is important to keep in mind that there are two types of witnesses:

- A *fact witness* [percipient witness]: someone who simply states and relates direct observations.
- An *expert witness*: someone that is well versed in facts related to some science or profession that is beyond the layperson's scope of knowledge. An expert witness may render an opinion.

In the Anglo-American legal tradition, the courtroom is an adversarial arena. If you are called as an expert witness you must remain neutral, testifying to the truth as you understand it. You provide an opinion based upon your evaluation of the facts. Your opinion is your expert application of your scientific knowledge to the facts and your assessment of the issue(s).

Remember, the jury or the judge is the determiner of the truth. Your presentation is viewed as only an opinion. The jury will make the ultimate determination about disputed issues.

PREPARING FOR TESTIMONY

Your preparation for testifying in court begins with the initial phone call or letter requesting you to testify, or if you are a party plaintiff or defendant to a dispute. Remember the key elements in preparation for trial:

1) You must know the specific legal issue to be assessed (obtain this in writing from the attorney, if you are serving as an expert witness).
2) You must know the specific legal standard that is to be applied (obtain this in writing from the attorney; again, this applies to expert witness testimony).
3) Be certain you do not have a conflict of interest in accepting your role (as an expert witness).
4) Have a clear understanding of fees with the retaining attorney.
5) If serving as either a party plaintiff or defendant, be sure you have reviewed the case with the attorney, and be sure that you are well versed in the facts of the case so that when you give testimony you are direct with your answers.

Depositions

Part of the preparation for trial might come in the form of a deposition. Depositions are the method whereby information is put into court-transcribed form before the actual trial. The deposition is performed in the presence of a court reporter, under oath. The testimony at a deposition is essentially the same as in a courtroom. There are two types of depositions:

Guidelines for Courtroom Testimony

1) The deposition to preserve testimony: this is performed to preserve testimony in the instance where a witness may not be available for trial.
2) The discovery deposition: this deposition serves the purpose of gathering data prior to trial. This deposition is used by opposing counsel to assess a witness' strengths and weaknesses, to assess facts and opinions to prepare for cross-examination at trial.

Important: The deposed witness (YOU) must answer only the questions asked and this should be done as briefly as possible, while being truthful. DO NOT offer more information than the question requires. DO NOT DO THE OPPOSING COUNSEL'S WORK FOR HIM/HER. Never offer more information than is actually requested.

Once the deposition is completed and transcribed:

a) Read the written deposition once it is completed and assess it for any errors that might have occurred in the transcription of that document.
b) Re-read the deposition just prior to trial so you are keenly aware of what you said at deposition. The reason being you do NOT want to be caught on cross examination contradicting what you said in the deposition: you will be held to task for this unless you have already planned to explain the discrepancy prior to trial.

Courtroom Testimony

The courtroom is the arena in which the attorneys do their work. The attorneys ask the questions. The witnesses answer the questions. The witnesses are *examined* by the attorneys. There are two main types of examination and two subtypes. The two main types are *direct examination* which is performed by your attorney, and *cross examination* which is performed by opposing counsel. Your attorney may then perform *redirect* and opposing counsel may then follow up with *re-cross*.

Your attorney will begin the process by qualifying you as an expert witness. It is here that your CV (curriculum vitae/resume) comes into play. Your attorney will highlight your qualifications as an expert: your education/training, your experience/expertise, your publications and special endeavors. Opposing counsel will either seek to discredit your accomplishments, thus attempting to prevent you from being qualified, or opposing counsel will seek to have your expert status "stipulated" so that the jury does not hear all of the stellar things about your career. Stipulation means that opposing counsel essentially says: "Your honor we stipulate to Dr. So and So's qualifications and accept Dr. So and So as an expert." It carries weight for the jury to hear your qualifications of education, training, board certifications, publications, so it is in your attorney's best interest to have those qualifications heard by the jury. That is up to your attorney. Remember, you are there to discuss your evaluation and your findings based upon the law as it applies to the facts: your role is not to win the case. That is up to the attorney, not you.

Your credibility is an important issue to the jury. This is established by:

a) Your expertise being demonstrated through your credentials, training, experience (note above)
b) Your presentation on the stand as trustworthy: this is established by your appearance and demeanor
c) Your dynamic style as a witness

Your credibility is related to your performance in cross examination as well. Observe the following recommendations as a means of establishing your credibility and as a means of enduring the trauma and potential humiliation of cross examination:

Guidelines for Courtroom Testimony

- Dress conservatively.
- Speak clearly, loudly enough.
- Do NOT be solicitous or overly polite to either your counsel or opposing counsel.
- Give short/concise answers without hesitation.
- Give definite answers: do not hedge.
- Do NOT use overly formal grammar.
- Do NOT use *psychobabble jargon* or *medicalese*; speak in clear, understandable terms.
- In the words of Ralph Waldo Emerson: "Eloquence is the power to translate a truth into language perfectly intelligible to the person to whom you speak."
- Do NOT "talk down" to the jurors.
- Do NOT become adversarial with opposing counsel.
- TELL THE TRUTH.
- DO NOT BE ARROGANT.
- You are NOT a stand up comic. You are an expert witness. This is a serious legal forum deciding a serious legal issue – DO NOT ATTEMPT TO BE HUMOROUS.
- Do NOT answer beyond the scope of the question. You may divert your attorney's line of questioning and you may provide fertile ground for cross examination by opposing counsel.
- You do NOT have a feeling or an impression; you are NOT speculating; you have a professional opinion based on a reasonable medical certainty. (Remember: you are an expert witness!)
- Do NOT mention the presence of a defendant's insurance company at a civil trial. That could lead to a mistrial.
- Do NOT become sarcastic.
- Do NOT become defensive; there is no need to be apologetic.
- Do NOT guess at an answer. If you do not know an answer, acknowledge that.

- Remember: any documents you take to the witness stand with you are fair game for opposing counsel to examine and cross examine.
- Do NOT acknowledge a book as an *authoritative text* or *learned text*, for once you have, anything within it is fair game. Note that your knowledge comes from many sources.
  - If you have quoted from a specific text, note it is only part of your research.
  - Before responding to a question referring to a quote from a source, insist upon seeing the quote in context.
- If asked if you are being paid for your testimony respond honestly in the following way: "I am not being paid for my testimony, I am being paid for my time like the other professionals in this courtroom."

Cross Examination

The purpose of cross examination is to discredit you, your testimony, and your opinion. Remember: if you are asked if you are a professional witness, you respond by saying:

> "My profession is the practice of medicine. It just so happens that I am frequently asked to provide my expert opinion on such issues in court."

Do NOT become an advocate for the patient. Your role is to apply your medical expertise to the facts as they are and to give a medically sound response based upon your level of training. The role of the attorneys is to advocate for their clients and to be their gladiators in the courtroom arena.

CHAPTER 10

Malingering

In performing a forensic evaluation, an issue that arises is determining whether or not the individual you are evaluating is telling you the truth. For some individuals, the forensic pathway is one for the escape of certain unpleasant circumstances. It is for this reason that some individuals might seek to pervert your services for his/her selfish use in contravention of the service of medical practice and the law. Rather than seeking assistance for a veritable mental illness or deficit, the individual is actually feigning symptoms to elicit from you a report, deposition or trial court testimony that will give the individual the imprimatur of validity that actually foils the well tuned wheels of justice and equity. When an individual feigns symptoms to be in the sick role, we call this factitious disorder. The individual in factitious disorder is conscious of his symptom creation, however he/she has an unconscious need to play the role of the patient. When an individual presents with symptoms and he/she is not consciously aware of the creation of the symptoms, we refer to this as somatoform disorder. However, when an individual consciously creates symptoms of mental illness or physical illness for the purpose of monetary gain or avoiding an unwanted consequence, this is called malingering. There are five main reasons for someone to malinger:

1) The perpetrator of a crime may wish to avoid punishment by feigning incompetence:

a) To stand trial
b) Insanity at the time of the commission of the offense
c) Diminished capacity to warrant mitigation of the penalty/ lessening of the sentence rendered
d) Incompetence to be executed

2) One may malinger to avoid being drafted into the military or to be relieved of undesirable military assignments or combat duty.

3) One may malinger to seek financial gain from:
a) Social security disability
b) Veteran's benefits
c) Workers' compensation
d) Damages in a lawsuit for alleged psychological injury

4) Prisoners in a correctional facility may feign psychiatric illness to:
a) Obtain drugs
b) Be transferred to a psychiatric facility for more comfort or to attempt to escape

5) One may malinger to obtain admission to a psychiatric hospital or a Veteran's Hospital to obtain "three hots and a cot."

Of all the diagnoses given by psychiatrists and psychologists, the diagnosis of malingering is one that is given the least; when given it is done with reluctance. What is the reason we are so concerned about giving this label to an individual? This is the only diagnosis whereby we are actually calling the individual's veracity into question. In very plain terms, when we give this diagnosis, we are calling the individual a liar. This is a very powerful concept. Especially when we realize that in giving this diagnosis we are at risk of being sued for defamation of character, slander, libel. In a 1996 study performed by Yates, Nordquist, and Schulz-Ross in assessing the frequency of malingered mental illness in a metropolitan emergency room the following statistics were noted:

- 13% of patients were strongly suspected or viewed as malingering
- Only 2.6% of patients received a comorbid diagnosis of malingering; not one patient was given the primary diagnosis of malingering
- The most commonly suspected motives for the act of malingering in their order of occurrence were:
    a) Seeking hospitalization for "three hots and a cot"
    b) Drug seeking
    c) Seeking to avoid jail
    d) Seeking financial gain

What about the detection of deception and discerning prevarication (lying)? Let us look at statistics and facts about lying. In studies performed (DePaulo, et al., 1996) to assess lying it was found that:

- College students tell an average of two lies per day.
- Adults in the community tell an average of one lie per day.
- College students and adults stated that they lied to about one-third of the individuals with whom they interacted.
- People lie more often on the telephone than face to face.
- Three out of four lies are told to benefit the person lying.
- One out of four lies is told to benefit another person.
- Women tend to tell more other-oriented lies than men; women tended to tell lies that were not of a self-centered nature:
    a) Women tend to tell lies intended to benefit other people – lies to flatter, comfort, protect.
    b) Women lie especially to spare the feelings of other women.
- In general, people tell more self-centered lies to men and other-oriented lies to women.
- In general, people tend to use their lies to impress men and to shield and reassure women.
- Extroverts lie more than introverts (research of Kashy and DePaulo, 1996).

- Older people lie less frequently than younger people (Kashy and DePaulo, 1996).

In research studies performed by Kraut and Poe in 1980 and again by Hendershot and Hess in 1982, Detectives and customs officers were no more accurate than undergraduate college students in their judgments of lying based upon observing an interview. Only secret service agents scored better.

Ekman and Frieson in 1974 found that facial expressions offered the least reliable clues to lying:

- Facial pleasantness was incorrectly rated by observers to be associated with honesty.
- Feigned smiles are more likely to be asymmetrical.
- Genuine smiles, as opposed to the feigned smiles, involve the eye muscles in addition to the facial muscles (Ekman, Friesen, and O'Sullivan, 1988).

McClintock and Hunt in 1975 noted that the individual who demonstrated a very calm facial visage belied his prevarication by limb movement.

In 1968 Maier and Thurber performed a study to determine whether people detect lying best by viewing the speaker, by merely listening, or by viewing and listening. The test was performed via:

1) Watching and hearing a videotaped interview.
2) Listening to the tape recording of the interview.
3) Reading a transcript of the interview.

Who do you think were best able to pick up the cues and clues of lying? If you guessed the individuals who both saw the tape and watched the individual you just got fooled. The audio listeners and transcript readers were the better judges of lying than the videotape watchers. The reason? The visual cues were the greatest distractors. DePaulo and his group of researchers reaffirmed this in 1980: attention to voice rather than visual cues and clues improves lie detection. The reason that might be? We are taught from early in our lives to maintain a poker face. We are taught not to become too facially exuberant when playing a game of cards or others will know what we hold in our hand. We carry this forward into our adult lives. Given that fact, what clues and cues can we look to in assisting our deciphering prevarication? Well, here is a small list:

- When people lie, they tend to speak in a higher pitched tone.
- When people lie, they tend to speak with more hesitant answers.
- When people lie, they tend to make more grammatical errors.
- When people lie, they tend to have more slips of the tongue.
- When people lie, they tend to make more negative statements (perhaps due to a sense of guilt?).
- When people lie, they tend to make more irrelevant statements, especially in response to a specific question.
- When people lie, they tend to make more over-generalized and/or vague statements.
- When people lie, they tend to demonstrate more self-manipulating gestures: such as rubbing or scratching.
- When people lie, they tend to use more passive rather than active forms of sentence structure; hedging-type statements.
- When people lie, watch for discrepancies between verbal and non-verbal communications.
- When people lie, their pupils dilate.
- When people lie, their answers seem more rehearsed than truthful statements.

Contrary to popular belief, liars do NOT demonstrate less eye contact with interviewers (Burns and Kints, 1970).

Liars do NOT have shifty eyes.

In assessing an individual for a psychiatric disorder, the better you understand the symptomatology of the illness, the better your ability to detect a feigned illness. It is harder to assess someone as malingering cognitive deficits than it is to assess a malingered psychosis. In malingering cognitive deficits one need only have to fail test items while looking like he/she is putting forth genuine effort.

What should you look for? In general terms, look for inconsistency in symptoms.

- Inconsistency in what the person reports: the individual reports confusion and disorganization in a very articulate and organized manner.
- Inconsistency in what the person reports and what you actually observe: an individual reports auditory hallucinations, yet during the interview he/she does not show any evidence of distraction.
- Inconsistency in observed symptoms: during the interview the individual behaves very confused and disorganized; later on the unit you observe the individual playing excellent bridge.
- Inconsistency between psychological test data and the individual's self-report of decrement.
- Keep in mind that true schizophrenics will demonstrate negative symptoms and malingerers will emphasize positive symptoms. Malingerers will emphasize their perception of what a positive symptom is.

In a study performed by Powell and his group in 1991 two groups of 40 individuals were enlisted: 40 true schizophrenic patients and 40 mental health staff members. The staff members were to malinger schizophrenic symptoms. When tested, the Mini Mental State Exam was used to test basic cognitive functioning. The malingering mental health staff

Malingering

members exaggerated cognitive deficits. It is commonly thought that if one has a mental illness that one's cognition is decreased. In reality, the schizophrenics did not perform poorly on the MMSE.

Most malingerers will feign auditory hallucinations. What do we know about hallucinations?

- They are intermittent.
- 88% of true psychotic patients report they come from outside their head.
- 93% of true psychotic patients report that the messages are clear and not mumbled.
- True psychotic patients develop techniques for lessening the voices.
- Both male and female voices are heard.
- 33% of the time, the psychotic patient will report the voices to be accusatory.
- 30% of psychotic patients will actually talk back to the voices.
- Visual hallucinations are found more often in malingerers than in truly psychotic individuals.
- True visual hallucinations are either of normal-sized people; alcoholic hallucinations may be of smaller people: Lilliputian hallucinations (think alcohol – these are rare in schizophrenics).
- Visual hallucinations are usually seen in color.
- Visual hallucinations are usually consistent with auditory hallucinations and with delusional thinking.
- Psychotic hallucinations do not change if the eyes are open or closed.
- Drug induced visual hallucinations are more easily seen with the eyes closed.
- Cocaine hallucinations are frequently visual and distinguished by shadows, flashing lights, and moving objects.
- Unformed hallucinations in the form of flashes of light or color may be seen in neurologic disease.

- If visual hallucinations occur in someone over the age of sixty years think eye pathology: cataracts.
- Dramatic, atypical visual hallucinations: think malingering!

When to suspect malingering with hallucinations:

Auditory
- If the auditory hallucination is continuous rather than intermittent
- If the auditory hallucination is vague or inaudible
- If the auditory hallucination is NOT associated with a delusion
- If the auditory hallucination is in stilted language rather than earthy language
- If the individual has NO strategies for diminishing the auditory hallucination
- If the individual claims he/she responds to all commands given

Visual
- If the individual claims visual hallucinations without auditory hallucinations
- If the visual hallucination is in black and white and NOT in color
- If the visual hallucination if very large
- If the visual hallucination is dramatic and atypical
- If the visual hallucination changes with the eyes closed

Clues to malingered psychosis
- Malingerers tend to overact their parts.
- Malingerers are eager to call attention to their symptoms/illnesses – they may even thrust their symptoms forward. When they enter the room, they may volunteer: "Boy the voices are really loud today!" Schizophrenics tend to be reluctant to discuss their symptoms and may even minimize or deny them.

Malingering

- It is more difficult for malingerers to successfully imitate the form of psychotic thought – the negative symptomatology, the perseveration, the disorganization; it is easier for them to mimic the content: claiming hallucinations, claiming delusions.
- Malingerers usually claim the sudden onset of delusions. In reality, delusional processes usually take weeks to develop.
- A malingerer's behavior is unlikely to conform to his alleged delusional thoughts; acute schizophrenic behavior does conform to the fixed, false belief system. Keep in mind however, that long term schizophrenic patients may no longer demonstrate agitation over their delusions.

Common actions to persecutory delusions are:

- The individual changes his place of residence.
- The individual takes trips to evade persecutors.
- The individual may barricade his room.
- The individual may carry a weapon for protection.
- The individual may make frequent calls to the police.
  - Malingerers feign the illness based upon their lay understanding of the illness.
  - Malingerers rarely demonstrate negative symptoms such as impaired relatedness, blunted affect, concrete thinking, peculiar thinking, and perseveration.
  - Persons malingering psychosis often pretend cognitive deficits.
  - Usually the malingerer will feign psychotic symptoms only when he thinks he is being observed or during the interview.

NOTE: persons who have true schizophrenia may also malinger auditory hallucinations or delusions when it serves them to escape criminal responsibility or to obtain *three hots and a cot*.

Methods to detect malingering:

- Gather as much data as possible prior to the interview.
- Obtain observations from staff.
- If this is a criminal defendant, attempt to interview him/her as soon as possible after the crime.
- Ask open ended questions.
- Do not give clues to the interviewee about what true hallucinations should be like.
- Review prior medical records to determine whether or not the individual has a prior history of mental illness and prior psychiatric hospitalizations.
- Obtain copies of all examiners' reports from the defense attorney (this should be done even when not suspecting malingering).
- Obtain school records, military records, and vocational histories (this will be especially helpful if intellectual disability is suspected).
- Find out if the individual has ever been around those with mental illness: could this be the individual's source for symptom feigning?
- If you suspect malingering, prolong the interview to tire the individual, for as malingerers become tired, it is harder for them to continue to feign their symptoms.
- If the individual claims to be taking psychiatric medications, request serum levels.

CHAPTER 11

Competence and Capacity

There are two key concepts to keep in mind when we as physicians are asked to determine someone's ability to make a decision affecting his/her health and medical well-being:

1) Capacity is what we as physicians determine
2) Competence/competency is what the judge/jury determines

It is important to keep in mind that competence (or competency) is a context-dependent term with criteria specific to the function (capacity) being evaluated. It is possible to be competent (to have capacity to perform) for one purpose, yet to be incompetent for another. Competence (capacity to perform) can also change as a person's underlying condition changes. The type of functioning necessary for a specific purpose generally involves intellectual and emotional capabilities that a medical expert may be most qualified to assess.

REMEMBER: A psychiatric diagnosis is NOT synonymous with incompetence. Only the manner in which the mental disorder interferes with functioning in a specified context is relevant to an assessment of incompetence. Often the law itself will specify the legal criteria for competence/incompetence.

When rendering a professional medical opinion keep in mind that value judgments should be distinguished from professional opinions and scientific facts.

AGAIN: Competence is based on the ability to function in a specified situation or task.

Some authors/commentators distinguish between standards for general and standards for specific competence. General competence questions are raised when it is felt that a person is unable to make decisions about a wide range of affairs.

A finding of general incompetence can lead to a person being placed under guardianship or conservatorship.

As noted above, specific competence refers to the ability to perform a specific function. Note that conservatorship is usually more limited than guardianship, which is more general. Also, keep in mind that if a person improves and general competence is restored, the court should be petitioned to rescind the guardianship or conservatorship.

It should be borne in mind that statutory and case law criteria for competence can be vague and allow for flexibility as well as subjectivity. An attempt should always be made to find out and clarify the legal criteria before offering an opinion.

Let us look at areas that you will be asked to evaluate. In your assessment, your report, and possible courtroom or administrative hearing testimony, you will want to cover certain areas (and to have read the relevant statute pertaining to the issues of competence).

CIVIL LAW

1) Consent to Medical Treatment

You will be asked to assess patients to determine whether or not they are competent to consent to medical treatment, or in the alternative, are they competent to refuse medical treatment. The two key issues that are of focus are: individual autonomy and rational decision making. The underlying fundamental question is: Is the (this)

Competence and Capacity

person capable of giving informed consent. This then is your task as the medical expert, to determine if the person is able to a) understand the particular treatment being offered, b) make a discernible decision one way or the other regarding the treatment being offered, and c) can the (this) individual communicate that decision either verbally or nonverbally.

2) Do Not Confuse Your Role

Your role is not to determine whether the physician gave the (this) person the appropriate information or data, rather, your role is to determine that had the person been given the appropriate data could this person have understood, made a decision, and communicated that decision.

Let us take an example: Assume for a moment that a 47 year old female with delusional disorder believes all her colleagues at work are seeking to poison her and the cook in the cafeteria is also seeking to poison her. She is able to go to work every day, she is able to pay her bills, she goes to movies, and she even goes out on dates, since she and her husband have been divorced due to her delusional belief. She is found to have a breast lump and is being confronted with the question of lumpectomy or mastectomy. You are asked as the medical expert: is this patient competent to make the decision she chooses. You will, of course, perform a mental status exam, as well as a Folstein Mini Mental Status Exam. What are the three key questions you must determine?

1) Does this patient understand her illness?
2) Does this patient understand the treatments being offered?
    a) What is/are the likely results of each recommended treatment?
    b) If no treatment is undertaken what is the likely result?
    c) On what basis does the patient base her decision?*
3) Can this patient communicate her decision?

* Note 2) c: *on what basis does the patient base her decision?* This is the pivotal issue with regard to this patient. Remember that having a mental illness in and of itself does not exclude someone from being competent. The patient with delusional disorder may base her decision on good medical understanding. If the patient meets the criteria of #1: understands the illness and #2: understands the treatments offered; understands the potential for metastatic disease if the lump is part of a malignancy and is not fully excised, and #3: is able to communicate this to her physician, she might prove competent. If however, her decision is based on all of the above with the added element that she feels the poison her work colleagues and the cafeteria cook are seeking to place in her food may destroy all of the cancer cells and thus she chooses no treatment at all, then you must reassess the extent of the mental illness in undermining this patient's capacity to make a rational decision.

CHAPTER 12

Contract Law

As a physician you will find yourself entering into numerous contracts. In fact, as a student you already have. You have entered into lease agreement contracts for apartment rental, contracts for the repayment of student loans, contracts for borrowing money for car loans, employment contracts. This list is endless. What actually is a contract? How does one make a contract? What does it mean to be an enforceable contract? A voidable contract? A void contract? A written contract? A verbal contact? Lots of questions about contracts exist. In fact, contract law is its own separate category. It is so important that in the first year of law school there is an entire, separate course taught on Contract Law.

What is a contract? A contract is a promise or set of promises, for breach (meaning failure to perform what you have promised to perform) of which the law gives a remedy (the means employed to enforce or redress an injury) or the performance of which the law in some way recognizes as a duty [from the Restatement of Contracts].

WHAT ARE THE TYPES OF CONTRACTS?
Based on Formation

- Express: an express contract is formed by language.
- Implied: an implied contract is formed by conduct.
- Quasi: these are NOT really contracts at all. They are constructed by courts to avoid unjust enrichment by permitting the plaintiff to bring an action in restitution to recover the amount

of the benefit conferred upon the defendant [the Court creates the fiction of a contract so that justice will be done].

Based on direction of benefit

- Bilateral: this is the traditional contract with the exchange of mutual promises; that is each party gives a promise to the other party. Example: Sidney promises to sell his Corvette to Henry for $35,000 and Henry promises to purchase the car at that price.
- Unilateral: the traditional unilateral contract was one in which the offer requested performance rather than a promise. In this instance, the person who makes an offer promises to pay a sum upon the completion of an act by the promisee. Once the promise is completed, a contract has been formed. There is one promisor and one promisee. Example: Sidney promises to pay Henry $50.00 if Henry will deliver the maintenance manual for Corvettes to XYZ Auto Repair Center. Henry is under no obligation to deliver that manual to XYZ, however if he does in fact do so, then Sidney is obligated (contractually) to pay him the $50.

Note: unilateral contracts are very rare, and under modern law they exist in only two distinct situations:

- Where the offeror clearly indicates that performance is the ONLY manner of acceptance.
- An offer to the public so clearly contemplates performance rather than promises (such as a reward being offered after the completion of a specified act).

Some contracts are valid and some are not; some contracts are enforceable, some are not. How do you know which is which? There are three main types:

Void Contract: this is one that is without legal merit at its inception. Example: an agreement (contract) to commit a crime.

Voidable Contract: this is one in which one or both of the parties may elect to void the contract. Example: contracts between infants (under the age of majority) and/or contracts of those with mental illness. A contract entered into by an infant (one under the age of majority) and an adult, while binding on the adult, may be voided by the minor if he/she so elects.

Unenforceable Contract: this is a contract that would be otherwise valid except one or both of the parties may successfully object to the enforcement based on the grounds of circumstances outside the contract that allow for it to be voided. Example: the allotted time for the contract has expired or the contract was made orally by and between the parties and the value of the contract exceeds the statutory amount for verbal (oral) contracts.

Okay. We've now touched on the idea of contracts yet how are they created? In assessing whether or not a contract has been created, the Court will ask three main questions:

1) Was there mutual assent? (*a meeting of the minds*)
2) Was there consideration?
3) Are there any defenses to creation of the contract?

MUTUAL ASSENT

Mutual assent is essentially two people agreeing to the same bargain at the same time. Put succinctly it is a meeting of the minds. The contractual process begins with:

- Negotiation, then moves to
- An offer, then comes
- The acceptance, then (and this is where law suits usually arise) comes
- Performance (or in the case of a lawsuit, the lack thereof)

Offer

The *offer* is presented by the offeror to the offeree. The offer, in order to lay the groundwork for a valid contract must create a reasonable expectation in the offeree that the offeror is willing to enter into a contract on the basis of the terms that he/she is offering. The three key questions one must ask to assess whether or not an offer creates reasonable expectation are:

- Did the offeror express a promise, undertaking, or commitment to enter into a contract?
- Did the offeror express the offer in certain and definite terms?
- Did the offeror communicate all of the above to the offeree?

Since this is a medical jurisprudence and medical ethics course, and not a first year law school course in contracts, I will not wear you out with the subtle nuances of the language interpretations of contracts. Suffice it to say, the language of the offer determines whether or not an actual offer is being made or whether one is merely setting the stage for negotiations leading to an offer. Certain words and phrases are considered invitations or preliminary negotiations for an offer:

I would consider selling for...............
I am asking $50 for..........(or best offer)

Of note: Advertisements, catalogues, circular letters containing price quotations are usually construed to be mere invitations for offers. They are announcements of prices at which the seller is willing to receive offers. In certain situations, courts have treated advertisements as offers where the language of the advertisement can be construed as containing a promise, where the terms are certain and definite and where the offeree(s) will be clearly defined. Example: A store advertised a fur coat worth $140 for $1 on a first come, first served basis. The court held the offer to be valid for the first person accepting on this basis as nothing was left open for negotiation.

An offer must be definite and certain in its terms. The terms to be definite and certain must contain the following (where applicable on the type of contract created):

- The offeree must be clearly identified: in the example above, it is defined by the first person to come in for the fur coat.
- The subject matter of the deal must be certain (in real estate the land must be defined clearly; in sale of goods the items must be clearly defined and the price defined).
- In employment contracts the duration must be specified.

For an offer to be valid, there must be a communication of the offer to the offeree allowing the offeree the power to accept.

Acceptance

The acceptance is a manifestation of assent to the terms of an offer in the manner prescribed or authorized in the offer. Thus, by agreeing to the terms in the offer and demonstrating that agreement, the offeree exercises the power given him by the offeror to create a contract. For an acceptance to be valid, there are three requirements that must be met:

- The acceptance is made by one who has the power of acceptance.
- The offeree has accepted via a valid mode of acceptance.
- The acceptance must be absolute, unqualified and unconditional in meeting the terms of the offer.

Consideration

After determining that there has been mutual assent: an offer and an acceptance, it must be established that consideration is present.

The basic question that a court will ask in determining consideration issues is what type of contract does the law want to enforce. In other words, is it willing to recognize a particular type of exchange as creating legal obligations? Basically, two elements must be present to create consideration:

- A bargained for exchange between the parties.
- That which is bargained for must be considered legal value: some *benefit to the offeror* or *detriment to the offeree*.

Example: John agrees to sell his motorcycle to Bill for $1200. In exchange for John's promise to sell the motorcycle for $1200, Bill promises to pay John the amount of $1200 for the used motorcycle. Both elements of consideration are there: John's promise induced a detriment in Bill; Bill's detriment induced John to make good on the promise. Therefore John's promise was bargained-for. Also: both John and Bill experience a detriment – John transfers ownership in his motorcycle to Bill, and Bill pays $1200 to John.

Defenses to Formation of a Contract

If both parties have a meeting of the minds (mutual assent) [there is an offer and there is an acceptance], there is consideration present, YET one of the parties to the contract has available and wishes to assert a valid defense to the formation of the contract, then THERE IS NO CONTRACT.

There are seven (7) major defenses to foil the formation of a contract:

1) Capacity of the Parties
   a) Age
   b) Mental Incapacity
   c) Intoxication
2) Statute of Frauds
3) Illegality

4) Misrepresentation and Fraud
5) Duress and Coercion
6) Mistake
7) Unconscionability

1. The *capacity of the parties* is important. If one of the parties to the contract is a minor, not having reached the age of majority, (note this may vary from jurisdiction to jurisdiction as essentially 18, 19 or 21 years of age), the minor may elect to disregard the contract, however the adult may NOT opt to void the contract. Upon reaching the age of majority, the minor may affirm the contract. There are certain exceptions to the voidability of the contract by an infant:

- Necessities: an infant is bound to pay the reasonable value of necessities. The definition of necessities is determined by the court.
- Statutory Exceptions: student loan contracts, insurance contracts.

Again, as with minors, those whose mental capacity is so deficient that he/she is incapable of understanding the nature and significance of a contract may disaffirm when lucid or by his/her legal representative. He may likewise affirm during a lucid interval or upon complete recovery even without former restoration by judicial action. Meaning: the contract is voidable. However, as with minors, mental incompetents are liable in quasi-contract for necessities furnished them.

An individual who is so intoxicated as not to understand the nature and significance of his/her promise may be held to have made only a voidable promise. There may be quasi-contractual obligation for necessities furnished during the period of incapacity.

2. The *Statute of Frauds* is a concept that applies to the enforceability and validity of ORAL CONTRACTS. In most instances an

oral contract is valid. However, certain agreements by statute must be created in writing and signed by the parties seeking to be bound. Again, as this is a course in medical jurisprudence and medical ethics, and not a first year law class, I will cut to the chase. As medical students, soon to be interns/residents/practicing physicians who may be entering into group agreements, furnishing an office, purchasing equipment, it is import to note that according to the Uniform Commercial Code §2-201(1), a promise for the sale of goods of $500 or more is not enforceable unless evidenced by writing.

Note also, that if a contract cannot be performed within one year from its creation, the contract must be in writing to be enforceable.

Goldman's rule of thumb: GET IT IN WRITING.

Also, note that if a contract is verbally formed, or if in fact no contract were made, however you have rendered services to someone for which you would normally receive compensation, you may still receive payment under the theory of *Quantum Meruit*, a legal theory allowing recovery for services performed for another on the basis of a contract implied in law or an implied promise to pay the performer for what the services were reasonably worth. It refers today to a theory under which a plaintiff may recover for reasonable value of services or materials furnished to another who has enjoyed those materials or services under circumstances that reasonably notified him that the plaintiff expected to be paid. This legal doctrine creates contractual liability implied by law, which arises not from the consent of the two parties, instead from the law of natural justice and equity, and which is based on the doctrine of unjust enrichment.

3. Some contracts are not enforceable because they are illegal. If either the consideration or the subject matter of a contract is illegal, this will serve as a defense to enforcement. Contracts may be illegal if they (are):

- Inconsistent with the State or Federal Constitution
- Violate a State or Federal Statute
- Violate public policy as declared by the courts

4. Where a party is induced to enter into a transaction with another party based upon the inducing individual's act of fraud or misrepresentation, the transaction is voidable against the inducing party.

5. Contracts created by duress and coercion, like those induced by fraud or misrepresentation, are also voidable and may be rescinded so long as the party has not affirmed the contract.

6. Contracts that are created based on mistaken identity, computations, valuations may be enforceable or voidable depending upon the materiality of the mistake, the party who labored under the mistaken belief, and whether or not there was any malfeasance afoot in the error.

7. A contract that is so unreasonably detrimental to the interest of one party may render the contract void and unenforceable due to it being unconscionable. An unconscionable contract is a bargain so one-sided as to amount to an absence of meaningful choice on the part of one of the parties together with contract terms unreasonably favorable to the other party.

THE XYZ MEDICAL GROUP, LLC
1234 Main Street
Any City, USA

MEMO TO ALL REQUESTING COPY OF MEDICAL RECORDS

In compliance with Illinois Revised Statutes 735 §5/8-2003-2006 as updated, The XYZ Medical Group, LLC, will provide medical record copies upon request for so long as required by statute and HIPAA, the request:
- Is in writing, and
- Is delivered (by United States Mail or in person) to the office of The XYZ Medical Group, LLC, 1234 Main Street, Any City, USA,

AND
- Is accompanied by appropriate consent/release form by the patient so requesting the documents

OR
- Is accompanied by a proper subpoena with necessary judge-signed court order in compliance with the Mental Health Statute for the State of Illinois

AND
- Is accompanied by the proper fee as so delineated by Illinois Revised Statute Chapter 735 Section 5 Paragraph 8-2006 Updated January 2010 and in accordance with HIPAA.

The practitioner shall be reimbursed by the person requesting such records at the time of such copying, for all reasonable expenses, including the costs of independent copy service companies, incurred by the practitioner in connection with such copying not to exceed:
- a $24.44 handling charge for processing the request for copies (HIPAA exempts patients from this fee)
- $0.92 cents per page for the first through 25th pages
- $0.61 cents per page for the 26th through 50th pages
- $0.31 cents per page for all pages in excess of 50
- the charge shall not exceed $1.53 per page for any copies made from microfiche or microfilm
- and actual shipping costs

These rates shall be automatically adjusted as set forth in Section 8-2006 and in compliance with HIPAA. The physician or other practitioner may, however, charge for the reasonable cost of all duplication of record material or information that cannot routinely be copied or duplicated on a standard commercial photocopy machine such as x- ray films or pictures.

Thank you,
The XYZ Medical Group, LLC Staff

INDEX

A

abandonment 35
Administrative Law 12
advance directive 25-27
advocates/guardians 24
American Legal System 9
autonomy 23-26

B

battery 36
Beauchamp, Tom L. 23
beneficence 25
bioethics 23
breach of confidentiality 37
breach of contract 37
Burden of Proof 20

C

capacity 97
Cardozo, Justice Benjamin 23-24
Childress, James 23
Common Law 13-14
competence 97-98
confidentiality 32
consent forms 53
Constitutional Rights 12
Constitutions 10-11, 14, 17
contempt 21
contract law 101, 109-110
  formation of a contract 106
  mutual assent 103
  offer 104
  types of conracts 101
  unenforceable contract 103
  voidable contract 103
  void contract 102
court of appeal 16
courtroom testimony 83
  cross examination 86
  depositions 82
  guidelines 81-82, 84-85
court system
  Federal 15
  State 15
cross examination 86

D

defamation 38
depositions 82
detrimental reliance 68
Discovery 22
durable power of attorney 27

E

ethical breach 32

F

Federal Appeals Courts 18
Federal Courts 13-14, 18-19
Federal Court System 17
Federal District Court 18

G

Goldman, David Eckstein 7

H

health care directive 27
HIPAA 78-80

I

informed consent 24, 44, 51- 53, 76
  causes of action 56
  duty to disclose 59
  failure to obtain informed
    consent 38
  landmark cases 44
informed refusal 24
Interrogatories 22

J

Judicial System 9, 14-5
justice 26

L

learned intermediary doctrine 32
living will 25, 27
locality rule 43

M

malingering 87-88, 92, 94, 96
  auditory hallucinations 93
  lying 89-90
  schizophrenic patients 92
malpractice 28, 32, 34
  abandonment 35
  battery 36
  breach of confidentiality 37
  breach of contract 37
  confidentiality 32
  damages 30
    compensatory 31
    punitive 31
  defamation 38
  dereliction of duty (breach) 29
  direct causation (proximate cause) 30
  duty 29
  failure to obtain informed consent 38
  failure to report 38
  failure to warn and control 39
  false imprisonment 39
  insurance 69
  locality rule 43
  negligent referrals 39
  statute of limitations 42
  strict liability 40
  vicarious liability 40
  warranty to cure 37
material disclosure 54
medical jurisprudence 23

medical malpractice insurance 69
  claims-made policy 70
  occurrence policy 70
medical records 61-62
  privacy and confidentiality 63
mutual assent 103

N

nonmaleficence 25

P

physician-patient relationship 66
power of attorney 24-25
privacy/confidentiality 25

R

Res Ipsa Loquitur 33
risk management 73
  communication 74

S

Schloendorf v Society of New York Hospital 23
State Courts 19
Statute of Limitations 42
Statutes 12
Subpoena 21
Subpoena Ad Testificandum 21
Subpoena Duces Tecum 21
Supreme Court 16, 18

T

tenure 20
tort 30
trial court 16
Truman v Thomas California Supreme Court 24

V

vegetative state 27

W

Warranty to Cure 37

www.ingramcontent.com/pod-product-compliance
Lightning Source LLC
Chambersburg PA
CBHW070946230426
43666CB00011B/2581